How ... mon... scho...

Are you wondering whether that avocado is ripe and ready?

Is that pork chop the right shade of pink?

How can you be sure a wedge of brie will "ripen" to your satisfaction?

How long will an open jar of strawberry preserves stay preserved?

For answers to these
and dozens of other
food questions, turn to
BUY IT FRESH,
KEEP IT FRESH

BUY IT FRESH, KEEP IT FRESH

The Complete A to Z Guide to Selecting and Storing Food

Joe Elder

FAWCETT GOLD MEDAL • NEW YORK

A Fawcett Gold Medal Book
Published by Ballantine Books
Copyright © 1990 by Joseph Elder

Library of Congress Catalog Card Number: 90-93046

ISBN 0-449-14640-5

Manufactured in the United States of America

First Edition: September 1990

This book is gratefully dedicated to
BH, ST, TM, and especially HP.

Acknowledgments

Though none of them is responsible for the uses to which I have put their data, the following sources have been most helpful in the preparation of this book, and I thank them.

Alaska Seafood Marketing Institute
American Dairy Association
American Egg Board
American Lamb Council
American Spice Trade Association
Beatrice Meats, Inc.
California Apricot Advisory Board
California Artichoke Advisory Board
California Avocado Commission
California Fresh Market Tomato Advisory Board
California Iceberg Lettuce Commission
California Kiwifruit Commission
California Pistachio Commission
California Raisin Advisory Board
California Strawberry Advisory Board
California Table Grape Commission
California Tree Fruit Agreement
Celestial Seasonings
Chocolate Manufacturers Association of USA
Cooperative Extension, New York State Colleges of Home Economics and Agriculture at Cornell University
Cornell Cooperative Extension/Orange County, New York
D'Arrigo Bros. (Andy Boy Broccoli)

Danish Dairy Board
Del Monte Corp.
Denmark Cheese Association
Evans Food Group
Florida Celery Committee
Florida Dept. of Agriculture and Consumer Services
Florida Lime & Avocado Administrative Committee
Frieda's Finest/Produce Specialties, Inc.
Georgia Peanut Commission
Gilroy Garlic Festival Association, Inc.
The Grand Union Company
Holly Farms Foods, Inc.
Idaho Potato Commission
International Apple Institute
International Olive Oil Council
Jordan Artichokes
Land O' Lakes
Maine Sardine Council
Maryland Seafood Marketing Authority
Michigan Bean Commission
National Broiler Council
National Fisheries Institute, Inc.
National Honey Board
National Marine Fisheries Service
National Mushroom Growers Association
National Oats Company
National Pasta Association
National Peach Council
National Pecan Marketing Council
National Pork Producers Council
National Watermelon Association
New Bedford Seafood Council
New Jersey Department of Agriculture
New Jersey Sweet Potato Commission
New Jersey White Potato Industry Council
New York Cherry Growers Association, Inc.
New Zealand Kiwifruit Authority
North American Blueberry Council

Northwest Cherry Growers
Ocean Garden Products, Inc.
Ocean Spray Cranberries, Inc.
Omaha Steaks International
100% Colombian Coffee Program
Oregon Wheat Commission
Perdue Farms
The Popcorn Institute
The Potato Board
Produce Marketing Association, Inc.
Rice Council for Market Development
Sunkist Growers, Inc.
The Sweet Potato Council of the U.S., Inc.
Swift-Eckrich, Inc.
Texas Fresh Promotional Board
Try-Foods International, Inc.
Tuna Research Foundation
United Fresh Fruit and Vegetable Association
United States Department of Agriculture
Washington Apple Commission
Washington State Fruit Commission
Western New York Apple Growers Association, Inc.
Wisconsin Milk Marketing Board

Preface

Although it had not yet reached the proportion of a major issue for me, along with life, death, taxes, and urban survival, I had in recent years become increasingly perplexed and thoughtful about fresh food, whatever that might be, along with ways and means of buying and keeping it in that happy state.

More and more often I seemed to find myself standing bewildered in supermarket aisles wondering if that avocado was ripe and ready, if those pork chops had been sitting in their Styrofoam tray a tad too long, if that wedge of Brie would ever ooze satisfyingly. With ever greater frequency did I gaze in confusion at my refrigerator shelves asking myself whether to keep or toss that hunk of cheddar with the fuzzy blue stuff growing on it, that jar of strawberry preserves that I opened two months ago (or was it two years?), or those stalks of celery that felt as though I could tie knots in them.

The food questions proliferated. Is this black avocado normal or what? How about this gray film on the cooking chocolate? Why do my mushrooms always turn slimy? What of these greenish potatoes? Are they a) very young, b) very old, c) moldy, or d) none of the above? Must I unpack all the eggs and put them in those little sculpted places in the refrigerator door?

As a result of such ignorance, I felt sure that I was neither buying food fresh nor storing it properly and, as a result of my when-in-doubt-throw-it-out policy, losing money as well. Necessity being the mother of invention, I therefore determined to write this book because I realized I needed it, badly, and assumed that many other people were in similar straits.

Although there is considerable debate about just what fresh food is, or should be, it seemed to me that, by definition, it almost always looked better, tasted better, was more nutritious, and even *felt* better, either in the hand or on the tongue, than foods that were somewhat less than fresh. As food lost its freshness, it seemed to look worse, taste worse, lose vitamins, and change in texture or consistency. In other words, it became yucky. But generalizations take us only so far. I needed to know specifics for a whole host of different foods. Could I look for the same fresh/unfresh signals in a honeydew as in a cantaloupe? In a winter squash as in a summer squash? In a fluke as in a flounder?

Another motivating factor behind the writing of this book was a growing awareness of health hazards in so-called fresh foods. *Salmonella* bacteria in fowl and even *inside* chicken eggs was pretty scary stuff. Perhaps there was nothing I could do about mercury in my sushi, other than to eschew the stuff (no hard task, that), but if food poisoning were a potential threat, I wanted to know how to avoid it.

The format of this book is very simple. With as little cross-referencing as possible, it offers an alphabetical guide, from Acorn Squash to Zucchini, to virtually all of the fresh foods commonly (and some not so commonly) found in our markets. You will not need to look under Fruits seeking information on Papayas; you will find them under P. Similarly, Hazelnuts fall under H rather than N for Nuts (although a general entry on Nuts does appear under N), Bok Choy under B rather than V for Vegetables, and so forth. Of necessity, we've made exceptions of Fish and Cheese. Because all fish display the same signs of freshness, or lack of it, and require the same kind of storage, one entry under F suffices for all. And because there are literally hundreds of individual cheeses but only a few basic types (such as hard and soft), one entry under C for Cheese proved the least cumbersome means of covering them coherently.

In addition to obviously fresh foods like vegetables, fruits, meats, and so forth, I decided to include as well a number of basic staples like ketchup, cereal, and mayonnaise that are found in every kitchen. Not "fresh" foods in the strictest sense of the word, we nonetheless expect them to uphold certain standards of what we perceive as fresh (as opposed to stale) quality. Although most of these processed and packaged foods have pretty fixed shelf lives in their pristine, unopened state, the question of how long and where to keep them after opening is not so easily answered. Thus, we learn that brown rice does not keep as long as white rice, that whole spices stay fresh twice as long as ground ones, and that good chocolate, under the right conditions, actually ages well for years like fine wine.

In my book, frozen food is not fresh food, but paradoxically, some frozen food may taste better than some fresh food. For example, if a pompano is quick-frozen on the boat, it's probably going to taste fresher than one that has been basking on ice for a week before you buy it, even though the latter may not be spoiled. On the other hand, freezing does alter the look, the taste, and the texture of most foods. They may be safe and tasty enough, but they aren't (strictly speaking) fresh anymore. Freezing might be the subject of another whole book, but, where it seemed appropriate, we did include some freezing tips on foods that don't require any special preparations and that emerge from the freezer relatively unscathed.

When does fresh become not fresh? This is difficult to say with certainty for every type of food. Obviously, a rotten egg is a rotten egg is a rotten egg. Most foods, however, deteriorate less dramatically. We provide fairly specific guides to storage life: "up to a week," "several months," "a year or more," and so on. Does this mean that after that time, the food will suddenly become loathsome and dangerous to eat? Not necessarily, but it does mean that the food will have lost something of its fresh qualities of taste, appearance, texture, and nutritive value. An opened jar of mayonnaise, for instance, may be safe for up to a year in the refrigerator, but will it continue to taste and look the same? No, after about six months there will be noticeable changes in color and flavor.

A word about that "cool, dry, dark" storage place that crops up with some frequency in the following text. Is it an unobtainable ideal? Not really. Kitchen cabinets are obviously dark, which takes care of one of our criteria. Heat and humidity are the real problems and may be avoided by a) air-conditioning and/or b) choosing a cabinet that is not directly adjacent to sources of heat and moisture such as a stove, sink, or radiator. If a choice is available, a cabinet against a wall with northern exposure is also to be preferred. Failing these precautions, some downward adjustments in storage time must of necessity be made in prolonged hot and humid weather.

Dating on food packaging is important, of course, and should be heeded. Especially useful are the "sell by" and "use by" dates. "Sell by" doesn't mean that you must deep-six the product if you haven't consumed it by the given date. Milk, for example, will keep up to a week after the "sell by" date, and most products will remain relatively fresh for several days thereafter. "Use by" dates are suggestions. They don't mean that you must necessarily discard the food if unused by that date, unless of course it's spoiled; but even if it isn't, it may well have lost something in flavor, texture, and vitamins. The date tells us to be aware.

It may seem a nuisance at first, but dating your own foods is a sensible idea and should become second nature. Both date of purchase and date of opening (jar, can, carton, or whatever) should be noted, perhaps on a small, self-adhering label. Obviously this isn't necessary in the case of a bunch of grapes or a pot roast that you know you're going to consume within a day or so. But for that jar of honey or box of Wheaties or sack of potatoes that may sit around for weeks or months, the dating game works. If you're like me, you won't remember.

Many sources have contributed to this book, but I am especially grateful to the food trade associations that have given so generously of their knowledge and experience. It came as

4

something of a surprise to me that a trade association exists for practically any food you can shake a spatula at, from garlic to peanuts to kiwifruit. Although their viewpoints are understandably rather partisan at times, their cooperation has proved invaluable in the preparation of this work.

It has been my fond hope that *Buy It Fresh, Keep It Fresh* would become as much a kitchen staple as peanut butter and peppercorns. Thus, it gave me pause recently when *The New York Times* reported that Department of Agriculture scientists had invented a sort of light meter (it's truly as big as a bread box) that could measure the ripeness of a melon. Depending upon how much of this near-infrared light the melon absorbed, the scientists could tell how sweet the fruit was. Experiments were extended to onions and papayas, and, we are told, peaches and plums are on the docket. In some science-fictional future, maybe we'll all cruise the aisles with light beams clutched in our fists, diligently zapping the produce as we tool along with our shopping carts. Until then, may this book prove a more practical and a constant guide!

JOE ELDER
New York City

A

ACORN SQUASH

Among the most popular of winter squashes, the acorn may be found year-round but is at its peak in the fall. Small, dark green, shaped like its namesake, the acorn may display a touch of orange, but all-orange squash is to be avoided. The rind should be firm and hard, and the squash should have a heavy feel for its size, indicating a moist interior. Look for a dull rather than shiny surface and a rind free from bruises, gouges, and soft or sunken spots. Acorn squash will keep for a week or so at normal room temperatures. In a cool, airy place, away from direct sunlight, with temperatures around 50°F (a porch or breezeway, for example), it will keep for one or more months. In hot weather, refrigerate for up to two weeks.

ALFALFA SPROUTS

Alfalfa sprouts are readily available throughout the year. The shorter the sprout, the more tender. Be sure they are moist and crisp, avoiding those that are limp or soggy or browning. They should also have a fresh, nutty aroma. Store damp, but not waterlogged, sprouts in a plastic bag in the refrigerator, where they will keep for a week or more.

ALLSPICE

Not a mixture of other spices, as its name implies, allspice is the dried berry of the tropical allspice tree. It should be kept with other dried herbs and spices in a cool, dark cupboard or pantry. Do not expose to light and especially not to sources of heat, such as a stove. Keep the container tightly closed at all times. Allspice berries, under these conditions, will retain their potency for at least a year or even longer. Ground allspice may last no more than six months. Fading color and aroma are sure signs that the spice is over the hill. A small, self-adhering label indicating date of purchase will help to keep track of shelf life.

ALMOND

Almonds are available year-round. The light tan shells of fresh almonds should be clean and free from cracks and other surface blemishes. They will keep well for up to a year if placed in a tightly sealed container in a cool, dry place. If the weather is unusually hot and humid, store in the refrigerator. Shelled almonds should always be refrigerated and will keep for up to nine months. Almonds will keep for more than a year in the freezer. See also NUTS.

AMERICAN CHEESE
See CHEESE.

ANCHOVY

Canned anchovies (fresh are virtually never found in markets) will keep for up to a year in a cool, dry kitchen cupboard. Once the can is opened, the anchovies should be used promptly. Leftovers should be transferred immediately from the tin to a well-sealed glass or plastic container and will keep in the coldest part of the refrigerator for about a week. Their heavy salt content helps to preserve them.

ANISE
See FENNEL.

APPLE

Because they can be kept for long periods in cold storage, apples are available throughout the year. The best, crunchiest, juiciest apples, however, are obtained during their peak harvest season, from late summer through the fall. The color of the apple should be vivid and appropriate for the variety you are buying. A pure red apple such as the **red delicious** is not necessarily the standard by which all apples should be judged. The popular **golden delicious** is yellow, and the **Granny Smith** is bright green, for example. Regardless of color, the apple should feel smooth and firm and should not yield to gentle finger pressure. It should be free from any breaks in the skin and from bruises. A bruise may be a soft, discolored spot or may be just an indentation in the skin that hasn't yet gone mushy. Brownish, mottled areas on the skin may not look perfect, but they generally have no effect on the flavor or freshness of the fruit.

For the first time, in 1989, the U.S. apple crop was not sprayed with the chemical agent Alar, a suspected carcinogen. As a result, some varieties of apple may appear somewhat more blemished than in the past, though their freshness and eating quality should not be impaired. Alas, however, some varieties like the ever-popular **McIntosh** may prove too hard to grow without Alar and be phased out eventually.

Because apples ripen quickly, they should never be kept at room temperature for more than a day or two. Keep them in a plastic bag in the crisper section of the refrigerator, where they should remain fresh and crunchy for two to four weeks, depending upon the variety. It's a good idea to check for and eliminate any bruised fruit before you store apples; it's quite true that one rotten apple can spoil the barrel. Apples may also be stored in bulk during cool weather in a garage, basement, or on a porch, but care should be taken that they not be exposed to temperatures below 32°F. If threatened with freezing, cover apples with a blanket or cardboard box until temperatures moderate. Apples may be kept in this way for several months.

Crab apples are very small and acidic and generally are used only in making jelly or otherwise in cooking.

APPLE CIDER

Fresh, sweet apple cider as found at roadside stands in the fall differs from canned or bottled apple juice in that it is less filtered and has not been subjected to pasteurization. (Supermarket cider most likely has been pasteurized and contains preservatives.) Because of the lesser degree of filtration, apple cider often has a cloudy appearance from the apple particles in it. Apple cider must be refrigerated to prevent fermentation. Otherwise it will turn into hard apple cider, a mildly alcoholic drink. When storing fresh cider in the refrigerator, keep transferring it to smaller containers as you use it up. A full container is exposed to less air and thus stays fresher. In this way sweet apple cider will keep well in the refrigerator for a week or two. Cider may also be frozen for up to a year.

APPLE PEAR
See ASIAN PEAR.

APRICOT

Apricots are a very delicate fruit that must be handled carefully. Be choosy when selecting fresh apricots. Look for smooth, plump, well-formed, fairly firm fruit of orange yellow to orange color. Avoid bruised fruit or that with a yellow-green tinge. Firm fruit will ripen quickly at room temperature, away from direct sunlight in a well-ventilated place. An apricot is ready to eat when it yields to gentle finger pressure.

Store ripe fruit in a plastic bag in the refrigerator, where it will keep for several days. Remember to remove apricots from the refrigerator fifteen minutes or so before eating. Like cheese, apricots have a fuller, richer flavor when served at room temperature. Since apricots do not lend themselves well to long cold storage, they must be enjoyed fresh during their relatively brief harvest season, in June and July. See also DRIED FRUIT.

ARTICHOKE

Artichokes are available year-round but are in peak season from March through May. Artichokes should be compact, heavy, plump, and have a consistent green color. Look for firm globes that give slightly to pressure. Fall and winter artichokes may be darker or bronze-tipped or have a whitish, blistered appearance due to light frosting. These artichokes are often considered to be the most tender and flavorful. When the tips of the leaves, or "scales," are hard or when they are spreading or separating, it's a sign that the artichoke is overmature and likely to be tough and fibrous. Avoid artichokes that show wilting, drying, or mold. Size has little to do with either flavor or quality. So-called baby artichokes are the same vegetable as the larger variety: their size is determined by their placement on the plant, down low among the shady fronds where they are protected from the sun. Sprinkle fresh artichokes with a little water, seal in a plastic bag, and keep in the refrigerator for up to a week. Freezing fresh artichokes is not recommended.

ARUGULA

Also known as **rocket**, this increasingly popular salad green is now generally available throughout the year. It has been likened to watercress for its leaves and rather pungent, peppery taste. The leaves should be dark green and very fresh looking, not excessively dirty, and with no wilting or yellowing. Store in the refrigerator in a tightly sealed plastic bag for no more than two or three days, and wash gently but thoroughly just before using.

ASIAN PEAR

There are many varieties of this Oriental fruit available in the United States, mostly from August to March. They may be small or large and vary in color from chartreuse to brown to russet. Sometimes called a **pear apple** or an **apple pear**, they are round and crunchy like an apple with a flavor similar to that of a pear. The best come into season in early fall. They should be very firm and juicy and free from bruises, cuts, and soft spots. Store in the refrigerator where they will remain fresh for many months.

ASPARAGUS

This harbinger of spring is at its peak of flavor and freshness from March through June, but because asparagus is widely imported, it is available throughout the year. Asparagus spears should be firm with tight, purplish-colored tips that come to a point. Avoid asparagus with tips that are spreading or wet. Select the greenest asparagus. The farther down the stem the green extends, the fresher the vegetable. (There is also a white variety, little seen in the United States.) Some prefer fat stalks, some thin; there is no difference in quality or freshness. Whatever your preference, pick stalks of similar thickness for even cooking. The stem end will be tougher and more fibrous but can easily be snapped off with the fingers. Ideally, asparagus should be eaten as soon after purchase as possible. To store, wrap the stem ends in moist paper toweling and refrigerate in a plastic bag for no more than two days.

ATEMOYA
See CHERIMOYA.

AVOCADO
Avocados do not ripen on the tree. They must be picked and held at room temperature first. Basically, avocados come in two varieties: the more familiar one has thin, smooth green skin and is generally available from November through May. From January to November you can find the Hass variety, which is characterized by a thick, pebbly skin that darkens from green to purple black as it ripens. Whatever type you buy, look for fruit that is free from bruises or gouges. Some stores offer labeled, preripened fruit, but most avocados are sold quite firm. An avocado is ripe when it yields to pressure from your hand when squeezed gently. If you buy firm avocados, just store them out of the sun at room temperature until they soften. To speed up the ripening, put the avocados in a paper bag and check daily until they are ready. When they are ripe they may be kept in the refrigerator for up to one week.

B

BACON
Given to rancidity and molding, bacon is quite perishable and should always be refrigerated. Be sure the product is well sealed with no tears or punctures in its plastic container. Unopened, it will store safely up to and a bit beyond the "sell by" date on the package. Once opened, continue to refrigerate, tightly reseal package, and use up bacon within a week. **Canadian bacon**, somewhat more perishable, should be stored no more than four days after opening. Slab bacon and **salt pork**, tightly sealed, will keep for several

weeks in the refrigerator. Discard if mold appears on any of these foods.

BAKING POWDER

An unopened container of baking powder will keep for up to a year on a cool, dark, dry shelf. Once opened, the main problem is to keep out moisture. It's a good idea to transfer the baking powder to a tightly sealed canister. Stored on that dry shelf, and resealed tightly after each use, baking powder will stay fresh for up to six months.

BAKING SODA

An unopened box of baking soda will keep for years on a cool, dark, dry shelf. Once opened, the important thing is to keep the baking soda dry. A good solution is to seal the whole box inside a plastic Ziploc-type bag and reseal tightly after each use. Baking soda, under these conditions, will keep for a year or beyond.

BAMBOO SHOOTS

Bamboo shoots are rarely found fresh in American markets. They are the inner white flesh of the young, green stem of the bamboo plant. Refrigerate in a plastic bag for up to a week. Canned bamboo shoots, like most canned goods, will keep for up to a year on a cool, dry, dark kitchen shelf. Once opened, refrigerate shoots in fresh water, cover, and change water daily. Shoots will keep this way for several weeks.

BANANA

Bananas are shipped year-round on specially refrigerated freighters to arrive at the market before they are fully ripened. Bananas, of course, continue to ripen at room temperature after they are picked. Fruit should be plump and firm and free from bruises. The color of the skin is the best indicator of ripeness. Color will vary from green to dark yellow with brownish flecks, according to the degree of ripeness. Avoid grayish yellow fruit, which indicates chilling injury. Ripen bananas at room temperature. When they are at the preferred stage of ripeness, eat immediately or store in the refrigerator. It used to be an axiom that bananas should never be refrigerated, but cold only darkens the skin while the flesh remains fresh and edible for several days. It's a good idea to buy bananas at several stages of ripeness, so that they can be enjoyed over a longer period of time.

BARBECUE SAUCE
Unopened, bottled barbecue sauce will keep for up to a year on a kitchen shelf away from sources of light and heat. Once opened, barbecue sauce should be refrigerated. It will keep there, tightly sealed, for up to six months. Leftover homemade barbecue sauce should also be refrigerated but used within a few days.

BARLEY
This grain, a relative of wheat, is sold in most supermarkets in so-called pearled form (with bran removed and polished). It may be of either fine, medium, or coarse texture. Select a bag that is free from tears and dust. It will keep unopened on a cool, dark, dry shelf almost indefinitely. Once opened, transfer pearl barley to a tightly sealed canister, where it will keep for up to a year.

BASIL
This popular, pungent herb is available growing in pots during its summer season, in cut bunches the rest of the year. In any case, the leaves should have a bright green color. (There is also a less common reddish purple basil.) Avoid wilted or yellowing leaves or those showing insect damage. If the stems are immersed in water, be sure that the water is also fresh-looking and -smelling. Place basil pots in a sunny

window and keep soil damp but not soggy. Cut bunches of basil should be placed in a glass of water like flowers in a vase. Change water daily and use the herb promptly. Refrigeration tends to blacken basil leaves, but for long storage, freeze fresh basil leaves in water in an ice-cube tray and defrost as needed during the winter.

Dried basil leaves are a pale reflection of the fresh. Keep with other dried herbs and spices in a cool, dark cupboard or pantry. Do not expose to light and especially not to sources of heat, such as a stove. The container should be tightly closed at all times. Dried basil leaves, under these conditions, should retain some potency for up to a year, dried ground basil for up to six months. When the bright green color of the basil becomes pale and dull, the herb is probably over the hill. A good sniff for the characteristic smell of the herb is also a useful check on its freshness. A small, self-adhering label indicating date of purchase will help to keep track of the shelf life of the dried basil.

BATATA
See BONIATO.

BAY LEAF
Bay leaves should be whole and, if you can see them, of a rich, mossy green color. Keep them with other dried herbs and spices in a cool, dark cupboard or pantry. Do not expose to light and especially not to sources of heat, such as a stove. Keep the container tightly closed at all times. Bay leaves, under these conditions, will retain their potency for about a year. Fading color and aroma are sure signs that the bay is over the hill. A small, self-adhering label indicating date of purchase will help to keep track of shelf life.

BEAN SPROUTS

Sprouts may be found almost everywhere throughout the year. Most common are **mung bean** and **alfalfa sprouts**, but sometimes those from soy beans are available. The shorter the sprout, the more tender. Be sure they are moist and crisp, avoiding those that are limp, soggy, or browning. They should also have a fresh, nutty aroma. Store damp, but not waterlogged, sprouts in a plastic bag in the refrigerator, where they will keep for a week or more.

BEANS, DRIED

Chickpeas (garbanzos), black beans, pinto beans, navy beans, lentils, kidney beans, et al.—there is a great variety of dried beans available year-round, and all of them have the same buying/storing requirements. Avoid buying dried beans in bulk. Exposure to light and air (not to mention insects) can lead to loss of freshness and nutritive value. Most dried beans are sold in sealed plastic packages. If possible, select those that have been exposed to the least amount of light. Look for consistency in the beans, both of size and color. Avoid small tears in the package and tiny punctures in the beans. Familiar brand names will usually guarantee beans of good and uniform quality. Once opened, transfer beans to a tightly sealed container and store in a cool, dark, dry place, where the beans will keep for a year or more. Under ideal conditions, they will keep well almost indefinitely.

BEANS, FRESH

See specific kinds of fresh beans: GREEN, LIMA, WAX, and so on.

BEEF

Beef is always available in many forms. The best grade is called prime, the next choice, and the third good. Prime, usually available only from fine butchers, is likely to be the

17

tenderest (also the most costly), but the others are certainly of good quality, too. Whatever the grade of beef, it should be a vivid red with white fat and springy texture. Eschew beef in a torn package or one with an accumulation of blood in it; meat in the latter may have been frozen and thawed or may simply have been sitting too long in its prepackaged tray. Though not "fresh" in the strictest sense of the word, beef from mail-order houses that has been properly aged, vacuum-sealed, and quickly frozen may actually be of much superior quality to the average store-bought variety. Refrigerate all cuts of beef promptly. Leave in their original wrapping in the coldest part of the refrigerator if you plan to use the day of purchase or the next. If it is to be stored longer, rewrap beef loosely in plastic or foil to allow air to circulate about the meat. Be careful lest drippings that might contain harmful bacteria fall on other foods or refrigerator shelves. Larger cuts of beef like roasts will keep for up to five days, but ground beef, or **hamburger**, and stew meat should be cooked the day of purchase or the next at the very latest.

BEET
Beets may be found at all times of the year but are at their peak in the summer. They may be sold either in bunches with their tops still attached or separate and topless. If the beet tops are fresh and crisp, it's a good bet the beets will be, too. Select beets with good shape and deep red-violet color. The skin should be smooth and unblemished. Smaller beets are apt to have better flavor and texture. Cut off the tops, if any, leaving an inch or two of stem, and refrigerate unwashed beets in a plastic bag for up to two weeks.

BEET GREENS
Available mostly in spring and summer, beet greens are the tops of red beets harvested while the beets are immature. Choose fresh, young, and crisp green leaves. Avoid any with

coarse stems, wilted, reddish leaves, or signs of insect damage. Keep in the refrigerator in a sealed plastic bag and use promptly, within a day or two. Wash just before using.

BELGIAN ENDIVE
This luxury salad "green" is misnamed. Its tightly packed clusters of white leaves are sprouted from the root of the chicory plant. It is also known as **witloof chicory**. Available in fall, winter, and spring, the cylindrical-shaped Belgian endive is best when firm, young, and plump, with unblemished white leaves that may be yellow (but not green) at the tips. The smaller bunch is likely to be the freshest. Store in the refrigerator, wrapped in plastic, for no more than a day after purchase, and wash just before using.

BELL PEPPER
See PEPPER (SWEET).

BERRY
Available primarily from June through August, fresh berries should be plump, firm, and full-colored for their type. All kinds of berries, except for strawberries, should be free of their leaf caps. Avoid any baskets showing signs of bruised or leaking fruit. Mostly very perishable, berries should be refrigerated and (with few exceptions) used within a day or two of purchase. See also specific kinds of berries: STRAWBERRY, BLUEBERRY, CRANBERRY, BLACKBERRY, and so on.

BISCUIT
See BREAD.

BLACK BEANS
See BEANS, DRIED.

19

BLACKBERRY

Blackberries may be available from May to October but are in their prime season in June and July. They should be purchased at the peak of ripeness and consumed as soon as possible. Examine blackberries carefully. They should have a deep, even, glossy black color. Look for berries that are dry and plump and well formed. Avoid those that still have green caps attached; they were picked too early. There should be no sign of mold, rot, and bruising or of seeping juices on the container. If you can't eat them the same day, gently pick over the berries, discarding any that are too soft or moldy, and store the remainder, unwashed, for no more than another day or two in the refrigerator. Spread the berries in a single layer on a paper towel and cover lightly with plastic wrap. Wash, again gently, just before using. The very similar **boysenberry**, **youngberry**, and **dewberry** should be handled and stored in the same manner.

BLACK-EYED PEA

Also called **cowpeas**, black-eyed peas are actually closer to the bean than the pea family. Rarely found fresh above the Mason-Dixon line, they are a popular vegetable in the South. Crisp, firm, full pods with no yellowing or wilting are most desirable. Use promptly or store pods in a plastic bag in the refrigerator for no more than a day or two. See also BEANS, DRIED.

BLUE CHEESE
See CHEESE.

BLUEBERRY

Blueberries are at their best during the summer months. Select berries that are plump and firm, with even blue color (a reddish tint is to be avoided) and a light grayish bloom. Avoid berries that are soft, damp, moldly, or otherwise bruised or damaged. An excess of small or green berries in the batch is also to be eschewed. Gently pick over the berries, discarding these undesirable ones, and refrigerate until you are ready to use. They will keep for up to two weeks in a firm container wrapped in plastic. At room temperature blueberries quickly lose their fresh flavor. They should not be washed until just before they are to be used. Blueberries freeze very readily. Do not wash before freezing; the blueberries should be as dry as possible. Place a layer of berries on a baking sheet and put directly into the freezer. As soon as they are hard, they can be packed in plastic bags or containers and will keep for up to two years in a home freezer at 5°F or colder.

BOK CHOY
This Oriental cousin of Swiss chard is sometimes called **Chinese chard**. Available all year, it has broad white or greenish white stalks with loose, dark green leaves. Select fresh-looking, crisp, firm heads with unblemished stems and un-wilted leaves. Refrigerate in a plastic bag as soon as possible, and use within a couple of days of purchase.

BOLOGNA
See SAUSAGE.

BONIATO
This sweet potato is very popular in Latin and Caribbean countries and is available year-round, especially in large Hispanic/urban areas. It is also called **batata**. Its skin is brown or pinkish, its flesh white and somewhat drier than that of the conventional sweet potato. As with all potatoes, look for unblemished, mold-free boniatos. Any exterior bruise is likely to affect the entire vegetable. If possible, store in a cool (55°–60°F), dry place for several months, but if they must be kept at room temperature, use within a week. Do not refrigerate.

BOUILLON CUBES

Store these along with dried herbs and spices in a cool, dark, dry place, away from sources of heat and light. Keep them in a tightly sealed container for up to a year.

BOYSENBERRY
See BLACKBERRY.

BRAINS
See VARIETY MEATS.

BRAZIL NUT

This native of the South American jungles is available year-round. One of the hardest-shelled nuts, the Brazil is also quite oily and given to rancidity. Look for clean, dark shells that are free from cracks and other surface blemishes. On a cool, dry, dark shelf in a sealed canister, under ideal conditions, whole Brazil nuts can keep for up to six months, but refrigeration will prolong the life of these nuts, whether shelled or unshelled, to eight or ten months. Brazil nuts, whole or shelled, may be frozen for up to two years. See also NUTS.

BREAD

Commercial sliced breads usually have a "sell by" date, which should be heeded. If bread is purchased at a store with high turnover of this product, it may be presumed to be fresh and will keep for several days at room temperature. If you expect to consume the loaf within this short a period of time, simply keep it in a bread box. For longer storage, refrigerate. Because bread tends to dry out in the refrigerator, wrap it tightly in plastic and it will keep for up to a week. Refrigeration also helps to inhibit mold. If mold appears, discard. Soft breads will also freeze well for up to six months. Hard-crusted French and Italian breads are more short-lived. Keep them in a paper bag in a bread box or cabinet and use the same day or the next at the latest. **Rolls**, **biscuits**, and **muffins** require similar handling and storage.

BREAD CRUMBS
Fresh bread crumbs will keep for up to two weeks in the refrigerator in a tightly sealed container or plastic bag. Dried bread crumbs will keep there for two months or for up to a full year in the freezer.

BRIE
See CHEESE.

BROAD BEAN
See FAVA BEAN.

BROCCOLI
Available all year, broccoli should have a firm, compact cluster of small flower buds, dark green in color and with a purplish cast. Stems should not be too thick or tough. Avoid yellowing broccoli. If the purchased broccoli is not to be used right away, it should be wrapped in plastic or put into a plastic bag in the vegetable bin of the refrigerator. Store unwashed and use within five days at the outside. Broccoli stems usually are tender, but when the vegetable has been grown during cool weather, the outer skin becomes tough. Remove a thin layer with the vegetable peeler before cooking.

BROWN RICE
Unlike white rice, which keeps almost indefinitely, brown rice, because of the oil in the bran layers left on the grain, will keep unopened no more than six months on a cool, dry kitchen shelf and only about two months after opening in a tightly sealed canister. Refrigeration is recommended in

warm, humid weather. When in doubt, refrigerate immediately after opening the original brown rice package. If even a trace of mold appears, discard. See also RICE.

BROWN SUGAR

Whether dark or light, brown sugar should be kept in a cool, well-ventilated kitchen cupboard. Once the package is opened, brown sugar has a tendency to get hard, sometimes very hard. To forestall this process, transfer the sugar to a heavy plastic bag, then place the bag in a tightly sealed container and refrigerate. If sugar still hardens, add an apple quarter or a slice of fresh bread to the bag for a couple of days. The moisture from the apple or bread will help to restore the sugar. It will keep almost indefinitely.

BRUSSELS SPROUTS

These tiny cabbages did indeed originate in Brussels, Belgium, several hundred years ago. Available from September through May, they are at their best during the cool fall and winter months. The most important things to look for are bright green color and firm, compact sprouts. In general the smallest sprouts are the tenderest. Puffy, soft sprouts and yellowing leaves are to be avoided at all costs, as is any sign of insect damage. Brussels sprouts usually come in cellophane-wrapped packages, permitting a view of only a few sprouts on top of the pile. If these appear fresh and firm, however, chances are the rest of the sprouts are, too. Remove any loose or discolored leaves, transfer sprouts, unwashed, to a sealed plastic bag; store in the refrigerator crisper for up to a week.

BUTTER

Butter should be cold and well wrapped, with no tears in the package, when purchased. Check the "use by" date, which should be several months in the future. Do not keep butter in the molded butter compartment in the door of the refrigerator unless you anticipate using it within a week or so. Otherwise, it should keep well in the main body of the refrigerator up to the "use by" date and for about a month beyond that. Unsalted butter will not stay fresh as long as salted, since salt acts as a preservative. Always keep butter tightly wrapped in the refrigerator to prevent its picking up food odors. For longer storage, butter freezes well: up to four months in its original package, nine months if double-wrapped in foil. Butter in a covered dish may be left out at room temperature for a couple of days, but beyond that it takes on a somewhat strong, gamy taste and soon turns rancid. **Margarine** requires similar storage and handling, though it will keep even longer, up to a year, in the freezer.

BUTTER BEAN
See LIMA BEAN.

BUTTERCUP SQUASH
Available primarily during the fall and winter months, the buttercup squash is of medium size, round, and green, with a prominent bump at the blossom (opposite the stem) end. The rind should be firm and hard, and the squash should have a heavy feel for its size, indicating that it is moist inside. Look for a dull rather than shiny surface and a rind free from bruises, gouges, and soft or sunken spots. Buttercup squash will keep for a week or so at normal room temperatures. In a cool, airy place, away from direct sunlight, with temperatures around 50°F, it will keep for one or more months. In hot weather refrigerate for up to two weeks.

BUTTERMILK
Like all dairy products, buttermilk should be purchased at a market with heavy turnover and "sell by" dates should be heeded. Store in the refrigerator and return promptly after

pouring, always pinching the spout tightly closed. Buttermilk will keep for up to two weeks. See also MILK.

BUTTERNUT SQUASH

Among the most popular of winter squashes, the butternut may be found year-round but is at its peak in the fall. Elongated in shape and buff-colored, the butternut should have no greenish patches. The rind should be firm and hard, and the squash should have a heavy feel for its size, indicating that it is moist inside. Look for a dull rather than shiny surface and a rind free from bruises, gouges, and soft or sunken spots. Butternut squash will keep for a week or so at normal room temperatures. In a cool, airy place, away from direct sunlight, with temperatures around 50°F, it will keep for one or more months. In hot weather refrigerate for up to two weeks.

CABBAGE

Whether green or red or of the curly-leaved **Savoy** variety, cabbages may be used interchangeably. They are available year-round. Look for heads that feel heavy in relationship to their size. If possible, select cabbage that still has some of its outer, "wrapper" leaves firmly attached to the stem. The stem should be cut close to the head. Avoid cabbage with wilted, decayed, or yellowing outer leaves, as well as heads showing worm damage. Look for good color, whether red or green. Cabbage without wrapper leaves will be much paler, of course, and not as fresh because it has probably been stored for a considerable length of time. Keep in a plastic bag in the crisper of the refrigerator, where red and green cabbage will keep for a week or more, Savoy cabbage for several days.

CACTUS LEAVES
See NOPALES.

CACTUS PEAR
See PRICKLY PEAR.

CAKE
For maximum freshness, cakes from a bakery should be purchased within a day or two at most from the time they were baked. (Get to know your baker.) As for commercially packaged cakes, check for and heed the "sell by" date, if any. At room temperature, cakes in their original box or otherwise covered will begin to stale after a couple of days; refrigeration will keep them fresh for only another day or two. Cakes with whipped cream or custard fillings should always be refrigerated and consumed promptly.

CALABAZO
This large, tropical pumpkinlike gourd may be found year-round, particularly in areas with sizable Hispanic populations. Similar to thick-skinned winter squash, a calabazo should feel heavy for its size and be free from cracks and soft spots. Store at room temperature for up to a week, and refrigerate only when temperatures exceed 75°F.

CAMEMBERT
See CHEESE.

CANADIAN BACON
See BACON.

CANTALOUPE

This popular melon may be found throughout the year, but the best are available from June until November. Like all melons, a cantaloupe should feel heavy for its size. A thick, raised "netting" should cover the entire skin, which should be of golden, not green, color. The skin, of course, should be intact and free from bruises and discolored areas. A distinct depression will appear at the stem end where the melon was detached from the vine. At this point, the whole scar should be smooth, well callused, and just slightly soft. A distinctive melony aroma can be detected in the fully ripe cantaloupe. Under gentle pressure between the hands, the melon should "give" slightly. If the cantaloupe has not reached this stage, let it ripen at room temperature, away from direct sunlight, for several days. It can then be refrigerated in a plastic bag for up to a week more.

CAPERS

Capers, the unopened flower buds of the caper shrub, are a common ingredient in Mediterranean cooking. Because they are pickled, they keep virtually forever in an unopened jar on a cool, dark, dry kitchen shelf. Once opened, they should be refrigerated and tightly resealed after each use. They will keep well for a month or two.

CAPON
See CHICKEN.

CARAMBOLA
See STAR FRUIT.

CARDOON

This relative of the artichoke looks like a very large, coarse bunch of celery and is a popular ingredient in southern Italian cooking. Cardoons may be found in fall and winter, but supplies and distribution are extremely limited. Look for crisp leaves and firm, though flexible, stalks. Younger, smaller stalks will be the most tender. Use promptly or refrigerate, wrapped in plastic, for a day or two.

CARROT

Carrots are available year-round, primarily in sealed plastic containers but sometimes in loose bunches with the greens still attached. If you buy the latter, remove the greens before storing. Select carrots that are firm, smooth, well shaped, and a rich orange in color. The more orange the carrot, the more vitamin A it is likely to contain. Wilted, soft, shriveled, or greenish carrots are to be eschewed. Also avoid carrots that are excessively rough or cracked or blunt at the ends. Small to medium carrots are likely to be sweeter-tasting than the larger ones. Wrapped in plastic, carrots will keep well in the crisper of the refrigerator for two to three weeks. Flabby carrots may sometimes be restored to firmness by soaking in ice water.

CASABA

A large, white-fleshed melon with furrowed rind and pointed at the blossom (opposite the stem) end, casabas are available from August until December, at their peak in the fall. The casaba is golden yellow in color when ripe. Avoid green casabas or those with broken rind, soft spots, or large discolored areas. Unlike other melons, the casaba does not give off a fruity aroma to indicate ripeness. The ripe casaba, apart from its golden color, should feel heavy for its size and give slightly to gentle pressure at the blossom end. If the casaba is not fully ripe, leave it at room temperature, away from direct sunlight, for several days, then refrigerate in a plastic bag for up to a week more.

CASHEW

This relative of the mango is virtually always sold in roasted/salted form and is widely available. Kept in a tightly sealed container in the refrigerator, cashews will last for up to six months. See also NUTS.

CASSAVA

See YUCCA.

CATSUP

See KETCHUP.

CAULIFLOWER

Cauliflower, a member of the cabbage family, is available twelve months a year but is at its best in the fall. Select heads that are white to creamy white in color with firm, compact florets, or "curds," and are free from excessive brown spots or discoloration. If the curds have started to spread, this is a sign of aging. The size of the head has no bearing on quality, but it should have a heavy feel to it. If the cauliflower still has its outer envelope of green leaves, they should also have a fresh, unwilted appearance. Wrap the head in plastic and keep in the refrigerator for up to a week. Wash just before preparing cauliflower for cooking.

CAVIAR

Truly fresh caviar (as opposed to that which has been pasteurized and vacuum-packed) is available in fine gourmet stores and departments. Always buy from a source that has heavy turnover. The grayish fish eggs should be shiny and translucent and fresh-smelling. Caviar keeps best at about 30°F. Store in the coldest part of the refrigerator. Tightly sealed, it should keep for several weeks, but after the jar is opened, consume the caviar that day or the next.

CAYENNE (POWDER)

This fiery red pepper is commonly sold in ground form and should be kept with other dried herbs and spices in a cool, dark cupboard or pantry. Do not expose to light and especially not to sources of heat, such as a stove. In fact, it is often recommended that cayenne, because of its natural oils, be refrigerated in the summer. Keep the container tightly closed at all times. Cayenne should retain its potency for about six months. Fading color and aroma are sure signs that the spice is over the hill. A small, self-adhering label indicating date of purchase will help to keep track of shelf life.

CAYENNE PEPPER (FRESH)
See PEPPER (HOT).

CELERIAC
See CELERY ROOT.

CELERY

Celery is available all year. When selecting celery, look for crisp, firm stalks that are brittle enough to snap easily. Select light to medium green stalks with a glossy surface that is free from rusty spots. Avoid wilted celery with cracked, bruised, loose, or broken stalks. The leaves should also have a fresh, green (not yellow) appearance and be no more than only slightly wilted. If outer stalks have been cut off in the market, chances are that the bunch is not the freshest. Wrap celery tightly in plastic and keep in the refrigerator crisper for a week or more. If celery becomes limp, it can often be restored by soaking in ice water.

CELERY CABBAGE
See CHINESE CABBAGE.

CELERY ROOT

This root vegetable is available throughout much of the year but is most commonly found in markets during the fall and winter months. Employed in soups and salads, it is perhaps best known for its use in a classic remoulade sauce. These brownish, dirty-looking bulbs with light-colored, crisp inner flesh should be firm and of medium size. Remove any leaf and/or root growth. The bulbs will keep for at least several days in the crisper of the refrigerator, and under ideal conditions, such as a cool, well-ventilated root cellar, celery root may be kept for months. Celery root is also known as **celeriac** and **knob celery**.

CELERY SEED

Heat, light, and dampness are the enemies of celery seed. Store in a cool, dark, dry place in an airtight container. Celery seed will keep there for several months, but because of its natural oil, refrigeration (especially in the summer) is preferred for longer storage of up to a year.

CEREAL

Most popular commercial cereals like cornflakes, shredded wheat, puffed rice, and the like have been refined and processed to remove the germ of the grain. Choose a well-sealed box or container, one free from tears, dust, or stains. Buying cereal at a well-stocked market with heavy turnover of these products will usually ensure freshness. The unopened box, kept in a cool, dark, dry place, will be fine for a year or more. Once opened, the ideal, if impractical, solution is to transfer the contents to a tightly sealed canister, in which the cereal will keep well, protected from moisture and insects, for six months or more. Otherwise, fold back the inner liner and reseal the box after each use, and return to that cool, dark, dry place: the cereal will keep for about three months under these conditions. Whole-grain cereals, or **groats**, on the other hand, do contain the oily germ and are prone to rancidity. If not used immediately, store these in a tightly sealed container in the refrigerator, where they will keep for several months.

CHARD
See SWISS CHARD.

CHAYOTE
This unusual tropical squash (also called **vegetable pear**) is gaining in popularity and may be found year-round in some retail outlets, especially in large urban areas. It is most abundant in the winter. In Cajun cooking, it is known as the **mirliton**. Oval or pear-shaped, the chayote is usually green in color but may be white; its waxy skin may be smooth or ribbed. Unlike common squashes, the chayote has just one large seed. As with other thin-skinned summer squashes, select firm vegetables that are free from bruises, gouges, and soft spots. Smaller chayotes are apt to be the tenderest. Stored in the refrigerator in a plastic bag, chayotes will keep for a few weeks.

CHEESE
Of first importance in the selection of cheese is the source. The freshest, highest-quality cheese is usually found in a gourmet shop that specializes in cheese or has a thriving cheese department. The gourmet department of a large department store may also stock a fine selection of quality cheeses. Know your source. Are the premises clean? Is most of the cheese kept cool or refrigerated? Is there a large turnover of product? Is tasting encouraged? A ''yes'' to each of these questions will generally ensure that you are buying fine cheese that will store well at home.

PROCESSED CHEESE, including the popular **American** as well as various cheese spreads, has been pasteurized or in

33

some way treated to prevent it from further ripening. What you see is what you get. Be sure that these products are well sealed when you buy them and, if you can see it, that the cheese is firm, shiny, and free from specks of mold. Avoid any that looks dried out or is curling or brownish around the edges. Most processed cheeses are dated and will keep for many months, unopened, either in the refrigerator or (check label) on a cool, dry shelf. After opening, unused portions, tightly sealed in foil or plastic, will keep for several more weeks in the refrigerator.

FRESH CHEESE, such as **cottage**, **cream**, **ricotta**, and **mozzarella**, is the most simple and perishable in this food category. Heed dating advice on the package, refrigerate, and use within a week of opening. (Fresh mozzarella should be consumed within a couple of days.) Keep tightly wrapped or covered to seal in moisture and keep out food odors. Store in the coldest part of the refrigerator.

SOFT CHEESE encompasses many varieties, including the familiar **Brie** and **Camembert**, the rich double and triple **crèmes**, and goat cheese. Usually sold in plastic-wrapped wedges, Brie and Camembert should have a plump, satiny look as if on the verge of ripeness. They may be stored for a few days in the refrigerator or left at room temperature to fully ripen overnight. Once ripe, do not return to the refrigerator; cover with plastic and consume leftover cheese within twenty-four hours. The crèmes will store for up to a week in the refrigerator and may be brought to room temperature more than once. **Goat cheese** keeps for a month or more in the refrigerator depending on how you like it: the older, the more pungent. Keep it tightly wrapped, or wrap and seal inside a glass container to keep odor *in*.

Other cheese types include HARD (**Parmesan** and **Romano**), FIRM (**Cheddar**, **Gouda**, **Swiss**), and SEMIFIRM (**Havarti**, **Muenster**, **Monterey Jack**). These all tend to last longer than their softer cousins but still need to be refrigerated. Wrap tightly in plastic or foil to seal in moisture. Ideal temperatures for these are 35°– 40°F, which may be obtained on the top shelf of the refrigerator or in a special cheese compartment. Some cheese experts wrap these types in a damp cloth before sealing with plastic or foil. Others run the flat of a knife over the cut side of the cheese or even spread a thin layer of butter on it, again to keep the cheese moist. If possible, take out only what you need and reseal the rest. If mold appears on *hard* cheeses, don't simply scrape it off but cut it out to a depth of about an inch to be sure it has been completely eliminated. Softer cheeses with even a trace of mold should be discarded. Most of these cheeses will keep well for a month or two in the refrigerator, though the very hard and drier Parmesan will last for up to a year if well protected.

BLUE CHEESE, of which the most famous example is Roquefort, is in a category by itself. The blue veining is a mold that gives the cheese its distinctive flavor. These cheeses should look firm and moist with no browning around the edges. They continue to ripen, even in the refrigerator, where they keep for up to a month. Wrap them loosely in a damp cloth or keep under a cheese dome, as blue cheeses need air circulation for best aging and flavor.

Most cheeses lose texture and become crumbly when frozen. In general, firmer cheeses such as Swiss and Cheddar lend themselves better to freezing than the softer varieties. Double-wrap in chunks of less than a pound and defrost slowly in the refrigerator before using. The Danish Dairy Board recommends that no cheese be kept frozen longer than three or four months and that blue and cream cheese not be frozen at all.

CHERIMOYA

This heart-shaped tropical fruit grows in South America and is also raised in Florida and California. Known as a **custard**

apple, it is available primarily during the winter months. It has a scaly, olive green leathery skin that darkens as the fruit ripens. If it turns completely dark, the cherimoya is over-ripe. Its flavor has been compared to a combination of papaya, banana, and pineapple. Look for firm fruit, free from bruises, and allow to ripen at room temperature. It's ready to eat when it yields to gentle pressure. When ripe, refrigerate in a plastic bag for a few days. Its hybrid cousin, the **atemoya**, is available from August to November and requires similar handling and storage.

CHERRY

Cherries are in season from May to August, but at their peak in June and July. Sweet cherries should be bright and glossy, ranging from deep red to almost black in color. They should be attached to fresh, green stems. Avoid cherries that are hard, sticky, or pale in color. A few varieties of cherry, especially sour ones used in cooking, are naturally pale, but with sweet cherries, darker is generally better. The larger and plumper the cherry, the tastier it is likely to be. Pass up any fruit that is soft or moldy or that has skin that is shriveled or broken. Cherries should be refrigerated as soon after purchase as possible. Store them in plastic bags in the crisper, where they should keep for at least two days. Wash only just before you are ready to eat them.

CHERRY TOMATO
See TOMATO.

CHERVIL

A rarity in supermarkets, chervil may occasionally be found fresh in gourmet outlets. A more delicate and subtle herb than parsley, which it resembles, chervil's light green leaves should appear fresh and be free from yellowing and wilting. Use promptly, but if chervil must be kept, rinse thoroughly, pat dry with a paper towel, and keep sealed in a plastic bag in the refrigerator for a day or two at most. For longer storage, up to six months or more, freeze the leaves in water in an ice-cube tray and use as needed.

Dried chervil is a pale reflection of the fresh. Keep with other herbs and spices in a cool, dark cupboard or pantry. Do not expose to light and especially not to sources of heat, such as a stove. Keep the container tightly closed at all times. Dried chervil, under these conditions, should retain some potency for up to a year. When its color becomes pale and dull, the herb is probably over the hill. A good sniff for the characteristic smell of chervil is also a useful check on its freshness. A small, self-adhering label indicating date of purchase will help to keep track of shelf life.

CHESTNUT
American chestnut trees were largely destroyed by a fungus, but many chestnuts are imported in the fall from Italy and elsewhere and are available through the winter. Fresh chestnuts should be clean and of a rich, reddish brown color. Look for chestnuts that are free from cracks and other surface blemishes and that do not appear to be dried out. They may be kept in a cool, dry, dark place, where they will remain fresh for four or five days. Use promptly. Refrigeration is not recommended.

CHICKEN
Highly perishable, poultry is among the most common sources of food poisoning. Although some *salmonella* bacteria are found in an alarmingly large percentage of chickens that reach the market (as many as half, according to some estimates), illness can always be avoided by a) thorough cooking, b) proper storage, and c) washing hands, cutting boards, knives, and whatever else came in contact with the chicken, in hot, soapy water to avoid spreading bacteria to

other foods. The meat must reach an internal temperature of 165°F to be sure that any and all *salmonella* bacteria is killed.

The freshest chickens can be obtained at a poultry market, but most chickens arrive at the supermarket within two or three days of slaughter. It is sometimes difficult to tell if a supermarket chicken has been frozen and thawed. Some producers deep-chill their chickens, which results in a partially frozen bird. Check for signs of ice along the wings, backs, and edges. Look, too, for a plump yet firm body and for clean skin free from bruises, discoloration, and tears. If the breastbone is soft and springy, the chicken is probably a young one and tender. Skin color has little to do with freshness or quality: it is more indicative of what kind of feed the chicken ate. The important thing is that the skin have a bright, wholesome (as opposed to a gray, pasty) look. The same is true of chicken parts, which should also be well shaped and meaty.

If packaged chicken has an immediate strong odor upon opening, it may be normal; but if the aroma lingers for more than a few minutes, the chicken may well be spoiled and should be returned to the market. Chicken should reach the refrigerator as soon as possible after purchase, where it will keep for about two days. A whole chicken can be stored in its original wrapping in the coldest part of the refrigerator. Chicken parts should be rinsed, patted dry with paper towels, repacked in foil or plastic, and used within twenty-four hours. Giblets should be promptly removed from a chicken and cooked that same day. **Rock Cornish game hens**, which are very small, young chickens, **capons**, which are older chickens that have been castrated, and other fowl such as **ducks** and **geese** require the same care and caution in handling and storage.

CHICKPEA
See BEANS, DRIED.

CHICORY
Sometimes referred to as **endive** (though unrelated to the very different **Belgian endive**), this popular bitter salad green is available year-round. Its curly leaves should be fresh-looking, clean, crisp, and cool. Avoid dry, yellowing, or wilted leaves or those showing reddish discoloration of the hearts. Refrigerate in a sealed plastic bag for three to five days, and wash just before using.

CHILI PEPPER
See PEPPER (HOT).

CHILI POWDER
Whether "hot" or "mild," chili powder should be kept with other dried herbs and spices in a cool, dark cupboard or pantry. Do not expose to light and especially not to sources of heat, such as a stove. In fact, it is often recommended that chili powder, because of its natural oils, be refrigerated in the summer. Keep the container tightly closed at all times. Chili powder should retain its potency for about six months. Fading color and aroma are sure signs that the powder is over the hill. A small, self-adhering label indicating date of purchase will help to keep track of shelf life.

CHILI SAUCE
Unopened, bottled chili sauce will keep for up to a year on a kitchen shelf away from sources of light and heat. Once opened, chili sauce should be stored in the refrigerator. It will keep there, tightly sealed, for up to six months.

CHINESE CABBAGE

Also known as **Nappa** or **celery cabbage**, Chinese cabbage is available year-round. Looking like a kind of cross between celery and cabbage, it comes in bunches of white stalks with a ruffled edging of leaves that may range from dark green to almost yellow. Look for crisp, unblemished bulbous stems and leaves with no trace of wilting. Store in the refrigerator wrapped in plastic for no more than a day or two after purchase.

CHINESE CHARD
See BOK CHOY.

CHINESE PARSLEY
See CORIANDER.

CHINESE PEA POD
See SNOW PEA.

CHIVES

Chives may be found year-round in many retail outlets, either in cut bunches or (especially in the spring) growing in small pots. A deep green in color, chives should have a fresh appearance and be free from yellowing and wilting. Repot growing chives to a larger container, keep in a sunny window, and let soil nearly dry out between waterings. Bunches of fresh chives should be washed, dried with paper toweling, and refrigerated in a plastic bag for up to a week. For longer storage, up to six months or more, seal chopped and thoroughly dried chives in a small plastic bag and freeze.

Dried chives should be kept with other dried herbs and spices in a cool, dark cupboard or pantry. Do not expose to light and especially not to sources of heat, such as a stove. Keep the container tightly closed at all times. Dried chives, under these conditions, should retain some potency for up to a year. When its color becomes pale and dull, the herb is probably over the hill. A good sniff for the characteristic smell of chives is also a useful check on freshness. A small, self-adhering label indicating date of purchase will help to keep track of shelf life.

CHOCOLATE

Under ideal conditions—temperatures in the sixties, relative humidity below 50 percent—plain dark chocolate, wrapped tightly, may keep literally for years and actually improve with age as fine wines do. In most kitchens, however, ideal conditions are not available. Keep chocolate on a cool, dry shelf, where the dark kind (bitter and semisweet) will keep for a year or more, milk chocolate for about half that time. In warm weather cocoa butter may rise to the surface of the chocolate, producing a whitish film, or "bloom." Quite harmless, this may be eliminated by melting the chocolate. Refrigeration, though not recommended, may be required in hot, humid weather, but chocolate must be very tightly wrapped to avoid absorbing moisture and food odors. Prolonged cold will also make chocolate brittle. Filled chocolate candies, if they must be stored, should also be tightly wrapped in plastic and refrigerated, where they may retain quality for several weeks. Plain **cocoa**, in a tightly sealed container, will keep for about eighteen months on a cool, dry shelf; cocoa with milk products added, for about a year.

CHUTNEY

This relish of fruits and spices will keep unopened on a cool, dark, dry shelf for up to a year. Once opened, it must be tightly sealed and placed in the refrigerator, where it will keep for about a month.

41

CIDER

See APPLE CIDER.

CILANTRO

See CORIANDER.

CINNAMON

Sold in both stick and powdered form, this familiar reddish brown spice is derived from the bark of a tropical tree. Store with other dried herbs and spices in a cool, dark cupboard or pantry. Do not expose to light and especially not to sources of heat, such as a stove. Keep the container tightly closed at all times. Cinnamon powder may retain its potency for six months, the sticks much longer. Fading color and aroma are sure signs that the spice is over the hill. A small, self-adhering label indicating date of purchase will help to keep track of shelf life.

CLAM

Like all shellfish, clams are extremely perishable. You can buy them year-round, but the best are available in the fall, winter, and spring. Purchase clams at a market that has a heavy turnover of shellfish. Clams in the shell should always be alive. You can tell if their shells are tightly closed or if they snap shut when touched. Avoid clams with broken shells or even a hint of an off odor. They should also feel heavy for their size. Clams are best consumed within a day of purchase but may keep for a few days in the coldest part of the refrigerator. Discard any whose shells stay open when tapped. If you must buy shucked clams, be sure of your fishmonger and use very promptly.

CLEMENTINE

The clementine is the smallest member of the mandarin orange family. Most are imported from Spain and North Africa and are in season from November until February. This tiny hybrid between the tangerine and other citrus varieties looks like a miniature tangerine and is equally easy to peel and segment. It is sweet and relatively free of seeds. Look for a bright orange color and a glossy skin free from blemishes, soft spots, and mold. As with all citrus fruit, the clementine with the most juice will have a heavy feel for its size. Clementines will keep at room temperature, away from heat and direct sunlight, for a week or more and in the refrigerator in a sealed plastic bag for several weeks.

CLOVES
A clove is a dried flower bud from the tropical clove tree and may be sold in whole or in powdered form. Store with other dried herbs and spices in a cool, dark cupboard or pantry. Do not expose to light and especially not to sources of heat, such as a stove. Keep the container tightly closed at all times. Ground cloves may retain potency for up to six months, the whole cloves for a year or more. Fading color and aroma are sure signs that the spice is over the hill. A small, self-adhering label indicating date of purchase will help to keep track of shelf life.

COCOA
See CHOCOLATE.

COCONUT
Fresh coconuts are available year-round but are in peak season from October through December. Avoid cracked shells or dampness around the "eyes" (those three small depressions found at one end of the shell). Shake the coconut before purchasing; you should hear the liquid sloshing about inside. The coconut should also feel heavy for its size. Unless weather is very warm, coconuts may be kept at room temperature for about two months. Unused portions, wrapped

tightly in plastic, will keep for about a week in the refrigerator. Coconut milk (more accurately called coconut water) will also keep in the refrigerator in a tightly sealed container for about a week. Shredded or flaked coconut, either canned or in plastic envelopes, will keep unopened for up to six months in a cool, dry kitchen cupboard. Refrigerate leftovers in a tightly sealed glass or plastic container. The moister, canned variety will keep for about a week, the drier coconut from a plastic envelope for up to a month.

COFFEE

Canned ground coffee purchased at the supermarket may be presumed to be fresh and should remain so for at least six months after purchase. Once the can is opened, however, the freshness will last for only a week or so at room temperature. Ground coffee will keep longer, up to a month, in the freezer. The only drawback here is that moisture tends to condense inside the can when it is removed from the freezer into warm air, so it makes sense to return the sealed can as promptly as possible. If the ground coffee comes in a paper or foil package, either transfer it to a tightly sealed container or put the whole package inside a self-sealing plastic bag. The freshest coffee is made from whole roasted coffee beans, but it will be no fresher than the beans themselves. They should have a rich, dark brown, glossy appearance; if they look dull in finish, they are probably old. Generally speaking, coffee beans sold in bulk in open barrels should be avoided unless you know that the retailer sells a great volume of them and restocks frequently. Store the beans in a tightly sealed container in the freezer, where they will retain freshness for up to three months. Again, to minimize condensation of moisture, take what you need and return the container promptly.

Instant coffee, unopened, keeps for up to a year in a cool, dry place and for several months after it is opened in that same place. If the weather is particularly warm and humid, refrigeration is recommended.

COLD CUTS
Cold cuts are quite perishable. Be sure the package is well sealed, with no tears or punctures, and that the meat inside looks moist and appealing. Faded color and dried edges should be avoided. Cold cuts will store well in the refrigerator up to and a week beyond the "sell by" date on the package; once opened, reseal tightly and use within a few days. Deli cold cuts, either in bulk or sliced, should also be tightly wrapped in plastic refrigerated, and consumed within two or three days. Discard if even a trace of mold appears.

COLLARD GREENS
Also known as just plain collards, these leafy greens are a traditional cooked vegetable in the South. They are available throughout the year in areas where they are popular. Choose fresh, young, and crisp green leaves. Avoid any with coarse stems, wilted, yellowing leaves, or signs of insect damage. Keep in the refrigerator in a sealed plastic bag, and use promptly within a day or two. Wash just before using.

COMINO
See CUMIN.

CONSERVES
See PRESERVES.

COOKIE
For maximum freshness, cookies from a bakery should be purchased within a day or two at most from the time they were baked. (Get to know your baker.) As for commercially packaged cookies, check for and heed the "sell by" date, if any. When you get them home and open the package, an old-

45

fashioned cookie jar or any other tightly sealed container will keep loose cookies relatively fresh for up to two weeks. In very warm and humid weather, refrigeration in a well-sealed container will keep them somewhat crisper. Most cookies also freeze well for up to a year.

COOKING OIL
See OIL, COOKING.

CORIANDER
Similar in appearance to Italian, or flat-leaf, parsley, fresh coriander may be found year-round in many retail outlets. It is well known as both **cilantro** and **Chinese parsley**. Its bright green leaves should be fresh-appearing and free from yellowing or wilting. If the stems are immersed in water, be sure that the water is also fresh-looking and -smelling. Rinse thoroughly and pat dry with a paper towel. Place the bunch of coriander in a drinking glass with stems immersed in two inches of water, then cover loosely with a plastic bag. Kept in the refrigerator in this manner, the coriander may stay fresh for several weeks. Check the water occasionally and replace if it appears cloudy. Do not keep coriander in the coldest part of the refrigerator, where it may become frost-bitten. For longest storage, chop coriander, dry thoroughly, place in plastic bags, and freeze for up to six months or longer.

Ground coriander and coriander seeds should be kept with other dried herbs and spices in a cool, dark cupboard or pantry. Do not expose to light and especially not to sources of heat, such as a stove. Keep the container tightly closed at all times. Coriander seeds, under these conditions, should retain potency for a year or more, the ground form for about six months. When the color of the coriander becomes pale and dull, it is probably over the hill. A good sniff for the characteristic smell of the herb is also a useful check on its freshness. A small, self-adhering label indicating date of purchase will help to keep track of the shelf life of the dried coriander.

CORN

The best advice about storing corn is—don't. Ideally, fresh, sweet corn should be rushed from field to boiling pot, but of course this is not always practical. Select corn with bright green, snug husks, with no signs of yellowing or drying, and moist, golden-brown silks. Whether the corn be yellow or white, look for even rows of plump, milky kernels just firm enough to offer slight resistance to pressure. Overmature corn is identified by large, excessively firm kernels, which are usually deeper in color than kernels at the most desirable stage of maturity. Do not select corn that feels warm to the touch. Once corn is picked, its sugars immediately start turning to starch. This process can be slowed down by lowering the temperature, so do refrigerate fresh corn as quickly as possible and use the same day. If this is impossible, remove the husks and silks, dip corn in a cold water bath, and wrap with plastic wrap. Store in the crisper of the refrigerator and use within two days at the most. The freshest sweet corn is, of course, that bought locally during the summer months. Available year-round, supermarket corn, if it has been properly cooled and shipped quickly to the store, may be reasonably fresh tasting.

CORN OIL
See OIL, COOKING.

CORN SALAD
See LAMB'S LETTUCE.

CORN SYRUP

Both light and dark corn syrup as well as so-called **pancake syrup** should be kept on a cool, dry, dark kitchen shelf. Heed dating advice on the bottle, if any. Unopened, the bottle will keep for up to six months; opened, for about the same length of time. Always reseal the cap tightly, and wipe thoroughly to remove any syrup residue that might attract insects. If mold forms on the surface of the syrup, discard.

CORNMEAL

Most cornmeals, whether yellow or white, have been refined, which means that the natural germ has been removed. Either transfer the contents of the package to a tightly sealed, non-metallic canister or seal the package itself in a heavy plastic bag. If properly stored in a cool, dark, dry cabinet, refined cornmeals will keep for about six months or somewhat longer in cold weather. A tightly sealed container is most important, as cornmeal is highly attractive to insects. Stone-ground and water-ground cornmeals do contain the natural oily germ and are therefore far more perishable. In a kitchen cabinet they will keep for no more than a month; in the refrigerator (preferred) for three months or longer.

CORNSTARCH

To keep out insects, store cornstarch in a tightly sealed, non-metallic canister or seal the package itself in a heavy plastic bag. If properly stored in a cool, dark, dry cabinet, cornstarch will keep for up to a year. It does eventually deteriorate, so check the package for dating information or date the box yourself when you buy it.

COS
See LETTUCE.

COTTAGE CHEESE
See CHEESE.

COWPEA
See BLACK-EYED PEA.

CRAB
Like all shellfish, crabs are extremely perishable. You may find them year-round near shore areas where they are caught, but they are at their best in warm weather. Purchase crabs at a market that has a heavy turnover of shellfish. If you catch them yourself, know the waters to be sure they are not polluted. Crabs, both hard- and soft-shelled, should be bought literally live and kicking. The soft-shelled variety (which is nothing but a hard-shelled crab that has temporarily shed its shell) should be soft, plump, and translucent. It is at its best in June, July, August. Very active crabs, stored in seaweed, may keep for a couple of days in the refrigerator but are best consumed on the day of purchase. They must still be alive when you cook them. Lump crabmeat is widely available and very perishable. Be sure of your fishmonger, look for snowy white, fresh-smelling meat, and store no more than a day in the coldest part of the refrigerator.

CRAB APPLE
See APPLE.

CRACKER
If crackers are purchased at a market with high turnover of these products, they may be presumed to be fresh and will stay so, unopened, for a good six months on a cool, dry shelf. If exposed to air and moisture, crackers go stale rather quickly, so once opened, transfer them promptly to a tightly sealed canister or other container and keep on that same shelf. As long as they remain dry, they will stay crisp and fresh for

a considerable amount of time, perhaps for several months depending on conditions and type. When crackers go limp they may be crisped up in the oven: spread them in a single layer on a cookie sheet and heat at 300°F for about five minutes. If crackers develop a rancid taste, they should be discarded.

CRACKER CRUMBS
Store in a tightly sealed container or plastic bag. Cracker crumbs will keep for two months in the refrigerator, up to a year in the freezer.

CRANBERRY
Fresh cranberries are in season from September to December. Select berries that are firm and plump and have a rich, glossy "cranberry red" color. Avoid berries that are soft, bruised, or moldy. Sort out any of these undesirable berries and store the rest in a plastic bag in the refrigerator for up to a month. Wash before using. Cranberries may be frozen directly in freezer bags and will keep for up to nine months. Do not thaw before cooking but follow recipe directions using frozen berries.

CRAYFISH
Like all shellfish, crayfish (or crawfish, as they are known in Cajun country) are extremely perishable. They may be found regionally where they are harvested from fresh water and should be purchased live and kicking. Cook them live on the day of purchase.

CREAM
Always select the latest "sell by" date and be sure the carton is well chilled and leak free. Whether light, heavy, or **half-and-half**, cream should be stored in the coldest part of the refrigerator, where it will keep for about a week. Return the

carton to the refrigerator promptly after using, and pinch the spout tightly closed. If the cream has merely soured, it can still be used to replace sour cream in baked goods. If the cream has really spoiled, its foul odor will give it away. See also MILK.

CREAM CHEESE
See CHEESE.

CRÈMES
See CHEESE.

CRENSHAW
Crenshaws are available from August until December and at their peak in late summer and early fall. This large (ten pounds and up) golden melon has almost salmon-colored flesh. Like all melons, it should feel heavy for its size. The rind should be firm, somewhat velvety in texture, and of golden color; green would indicate that the melon was picked prematurely, in which case it will not ripen further. Avoid crenshaws with broken rind, soft spots, or large discolored areas. The ripening fruit will exude a sweet, melony aroma. If the crenshaw is not fully ripe, leave it at room temperature, away from direct sunlight, for several days, then refrigerate in a plastic bag for up to a week more.

CUCUMBER
Good cucumbers can be found in the market throughout the year. When buying cucumbers, select those that are firm and of small to medium size, for these will tend to be sweeter than the largest ones. Look for a uniform rich, green color. The shade is important because the older the cucumber, the more likely that the color will fade to a dull green or even yellow. Also, older cucumbers generally have an overgrown, puffy appearance. Except in the summer, when local produce

is available, most cucumbers will be coated with a nontoxic wax, which makes them look shiny and helps to preserve them. If desired, the wax may be removed with a soft vegetable brush, or the cucumber may be peeled, though this will diminish its nutritive value. The small pickling cucumber known as the **Kirby** is a paler, whitish green and warty in texture. The large, ''burpless'' gourmet cucumber is generally expensive and bland in flavor due to its lack of seeds. Do not wash cucumbers before refrigerating. All varieties should keep well in the crisper for three to four days.

CUMIN (COMINO)

This common ingredient in both Oriental and Mexican cooking is sold in both whole seed and ground form. Store with other dried herbs and spices in a cool, dark cupboard or pantry. Do not expose to light and especially not to sources of heat, such as a stove. Keep the container tightly closed at all times. Because of their natural oil content, it's a good idea to store cumin seeds in the refrigerator during the summer. Ground cumin may retain potency for up to six months, the whole seeds for a year or more. Fading color and aroma are sure signs that the spice is over the hill. A small, self-adhering label indicating date of purchase will help to keep track of shelf life.

CURRANT, DRIED

Unlike the fresh currant (see below), which is a berry, the dried currant, like a raisin, is a dried grape. Used mainly in baking, it may be found in boxes on market shelves along with raisins. There are both black and white dried currants. Unopened, a box of dried currants will keep in a cool, dry place in the kitchen for up to six months. Once opened, keep the dried currants in a tightly sealed container in the refrigerator, where they will last for at least six months. If they become too dry and hard, they may be restored by running them briefly under hot water.

CURRANT, FRESH
This relative of the gooseberry is rarely seen in markets. It can be found, if at all, in June through August. Because of its tartness, it is used commonly in jellies and jams. The tiny berry is usually red, though there is also a black variety that is even more rare in the United States. (It seems the black currant harbors a fungus that is deadly to the white pine tree.) If you find currants, look for small, plump, dry berries of bright, red color. Stems should still be attached. Refrigerate in a plastic bag for no more than a day or two, and wash gently just before using. The fresh currant has nothing but its name in common with the dried currant (see above).

CURRY POWDER
A mixture of various spices, curry powder should be stored with other dried herbs and spices in a cool, dark cupboard or pantry. Do not expose to light and especially not to sources of heat, such as a stove. Keep the container tightly closed at all times. Curry powder may retain potency for up to six months. Fading color and aroma are sure signs that the curry is over the hill. A small, self-adhering label indicating date of purchase will help to keep track of shelf life.

CUSTARD APPLE
See CHERIMOYA.

D

DAIKON RADISH
See RADISH.

DANDELION GREENS
Dandelion greens are at their tenderest in the spring. If you cannot harvest your own, this bitter green is sometimes available in specialty markets. The slender arrowhead leaves should be young, crisp, and freshly green, with roots still attached. Avoid any with coarse stems or wilted, yellowing leaves. Store no more than a day in the refrigerator in a sealed plastic bag, and wash thoroughly just before using.

DASHEEN
See TARO.

DATE
Dates are usually packaged in plastic and may vary in degree of softness. Some may be pitted, others not. In any event, look for plump, shiny brown dates. Store unopened for up to six months on a cool, dry, dark kitchen shelf. Once opened, wrap the dates tightly in plastic and refrigerate. Very soft dates will keep for several weeks, drier dates for several months. If dates become moldy, discard. If they become too hard, they may be plumped up by soaking in warm water.

DEWBERRY
See BLACKBERRY.

DILL WEED
Fresh dill is commonly found in markets throughout the year. Its bright green, feathery foliage, looking like a more delicate version of carrot tops, should be free from yellowing or wilting. Rinse thoroughly and pat dry with a paper towel.

Kept sealed in a plastic bag in the refrigerator, dill should stay fresh for about a week. For longer storage, up to six months or more, seal chopped and thoroughly dried dill in a small plastic bag and freeze.

Dried dill should be kept with other dried herbs and spices in a cool, dark cupboard or pantry. Do not expose to light and especially not to sources of heat, such as a stove. Keep the container tightly closed at all times. Dried dill, under these conditions, should retain some potency for up to a year. When its rich green color becomes pale and dull, the herb is probably over the hill. A good sniff for the characteristic smell of dill is also a useful check on its freshness. A small, self-adhering label indicating date of purchase will help to keep track of shelf life.

DOCK
See SORREL.

DOUGHNUT
The "sell by" date, if any, should be heeded. Doughnuts purchased at a store with high turnover of this product may be presumed to be fresh and will keep for a couple of days at room temperature. If you expect to consume them within this short a period of time, simply keep them in a bread box in their original container. For longer storage, especially in summer or with cream-filled doughnuts, refrigerate. Because doughnuts tend to dry out in the refrigerator, store them in an airtight container or sealed plastic bag, and they will keep for up to a week. They will also freeze well for up to six months. Stale doughnuts may be freshened by wrapping loosely in foil and warming briefly in a 350°F oven.

DRIED FRUIT
Avoid dried fruits (prunes, apricots, figs, and so on) that rattle when their boxes are shaken. Remember that dried

does not mean dried out. If sold in plastic containers, look for bright color and a pliable texture to the fruit. On a cool, dry, dark kitchen shelf, an unopened package of dried fruit will keep for up to six months. Once opened, reseal the package tightly or transfer fruit to a well-sealed glass or plastic container, and refrigerate for up to eight months. If fruit becomes hardened, soak in warm water until plumped up.

DUCK
Not exactly commonplace, fresh ducks are increasingly available, especially in large cities, and require the same care in selection and storage as any poultry (see CHICKEN and TURKEY). Most ducks that reach the market, however, have been frozen. Be sure that they are frozen solid, with no accumulation of fluid in the package to indicate that the duck was frozen and thawed. Many have an expiration date attached, which will tell you how many more months the duck can remain frozen. Always thaw your duck completely in the refrigerator before cooking.

EGG
Among the more perishable foods, eggs will age more in one day at room temperature than in one week in the refrigerator. It's a good idea to make eggs among your last pickups at the market to reduce the time they are unrefrigerated. Once home, follow the rule of three C's: keep eggs *clean*, *cold*, and *covered*. Unless you've bought them fresh from the farm, eggs should not be washed before storing because washing removes the thin protective film or "bloom" that seals the pores, retains moisture, and keeps out bacteria, mold, and odors. Always discard any broken or leaking eggs, and re-

frigerate immediately, broad end up as they come in the carton. If you can, leave eggs in their original carton, which makes an excellent cover. Those molded egg compartments in the refrigerator are convenient, but they're usually in the wrong place to keep the eggs at sufficiently cold temperature. Use an inside shelf instead. Fresh eggs can be stored in their carton in the refrigerator from four to five weeks.

Of concern is the recent discovery of *salmonella* bacteria *inside* chicken eggs. Though perhaps no more than one in ten thousand eggs is so infected (the danger is much greater in raw chicken), it is recommended that the elderly and those whose immune systems are impaired or who are otherwise susceptible to food poisoning cook all eggs to a temperature of 160°F.

EGG NOODLES

Egg noodles, like most pastas, are made from flour and water, but obviously they also include eggs in the formula and, for this reason, are somewhat more perishable than simple flour/water pastas. There is little one can do to detect freshness in a package of dried noodles other than to be sure that the package has not been violated and that the place of purchase is one with high turnover of this product. Unopened, *dried* egg noodles will keep on a kitchen shelf for a month or two without undue deterioration. For longer storage, transfer noodles to a tightly sealed glass or plastic container, and keep in a dark, dry cabinet for up to six months. *Fresh* egg noodles are much more perishable; be sure that they were indeed made fresh very recently. Keep refrigerated and use within a day or two.

EGGPLANT

Excellent eggplants are available throughout the year. The common eggplant should have a uniform dark, rich purple-black skin that is unblemished and satiny smooth. Look for an eggplant that is firm and feels heavy in relationship to its size. Avoid those that are shriveled, soft, or flabby, as they are likely to be bitter-tasting. Those with symmetrical shape and a diameter of three to six inches are likely to have the finest, sweetest flesh. A bright green cap is also a good indicator of fresh quality. Eggplants come in a variety of sizes and colors (even white), including the small, slim Chinese or Italian eggplant, all of which may be judged like any other eggplant for freshness. Eggplants should be used fairly promptly after purchase. They will keep for a day or two at cool room temperature (60°F) away from direct sunlight or wrapped in plastic in the refrigerator for a bit longer than that.

ELDERBERRY

A common wild fruit throughout the eastern United States, elderberries are not sold on a commercial basis. The best way to enjoy them fresh in summer is to pick them from the shrub on which they grow. Unappealing as raw fruit, elderberries are used in jams and jellies and in making the famous elderberry wine. They should be firm, of a deep blackish purple color, and free from insect or bird damage. Use promptly or store for no more than another day or two in a plastic bag in the refrigerator. Wash just before using.

ENDIVE
See BELGIAN ENDIVE; CHICORY.

ESCAROLE

One of the bitter salad greens, escarole is available year-round. Its ruffled leaves shade from white to dark green and should be fresh-looking, clean, crisp, and cool. Avoid dry, yellowing, or wilted leaves or those showing reddish discoloration of the hearts. As with lettuces, store in a sealed plastic bag in the refrigerator for up to five days, and wash just before using.

F

FAVA BEAN
Also known as **broad beans**, favas are a rarity in markets but may be found in some areas where they are grown in spring and early summer. The large pods should be firm, crisp, of good green color and velvety texture. Pods bulging with large beans are overage and tough. *Eating raw fava beans is not recommended: they may prove toxic to some people*. Use promptly or refrigerate for no more than a day or two in a plastic bag.

FEIJOA
Native to South America, this tropical fruit is now grown primarily in New Zealand and is available in some retail outlets during the winter months. Look for firm, uniformly dark green feijoas, free from bruises and browning. Allowed to ripen at room temperature, away from direct sunlight, the feijoa will become soft and give forth a distinctive fruity aroma. When ripe, it can be refrigerated in a plastic bag for two or three days.

FENNEL
This rather unusual vegetable is often associated with Italian cooking. It is generally available from September until May. Fennel looks something like a bunch of celery with a rounded bulb at the base. Although the whole vegetable is edible, it is the bulb that is most often used in cooking or eaten raw. It is also known as **finocchio** or **anise**, because of its licoricelike flavor. Select fennel that appears crisp and unwilted.

The fernlike leaves should be fresh-looking and green, the bulb of medium size, well developed, firm, and white. Unless you are planning to use them for garnish, remove the leaves and store fennel in a plastic bag in the refrigerator for up to a week.

FETTUCINE
Fettucine, like most pastas, is nothing more than flour and water. There is little one can do to detect freshness in a package of dried fettucine other than to be sure that the package has not been violated and that the place of purchase is one with high turnover of this product. Unopened, dried fettucine will keep on a kitchen shelf for several months without undue deterioration. For longer storage, transfer fettucine to a tightly sealed glass or plastic container and keep in a dark, dry cabinet for up to a year. Fresh fettucine is much more perishable: be sure that it was indeed made fresh very recently. Keep refrigerated and use within a day or two.

FIDDLEHEAD
These delicate springtime ferns have a short season from April into June. Immature when harvested, they should have tightly furled fronds and should look dewy fresh as though they had just been picked. In fact, *do* pick your own if you can find them. Avoid fiddleheads that are limp, bruised, or dried out. Rush them home and use at once, or store them unwashed in a plastic bag in the refrigerator for no more than another day.

FIELD SALAD
See LAMB's LETTUCE.

FIG
Though dried figs are more common in the market, fresh ones do show up in some areas from June through Novem-

ber. They may be light (green to yellow) or dark (purple to black) in color. They should be soft but not mushy while still retaining their shape. Look for unblemished skins and fragrant aroma. A bit of light sugar at the blossom end is not unusual in a ripe fig, but avoid those that are oozing juices. Fragile and easily bruised, figs should be consumed promptly or stored no more than a day or two in a plastic bag in the refrigerator.

FILBERT
See HAZELNUT.

FINOCCHIO
See FENNEL.

FISH
Fresh fish is extremely perishable and should always be refrigerated immediately. Avoid undue delays between point of purchase and home. Whatever the variety, whole fresh fish have certain characteristics that indicate freshness:

- Bright, clear, full eyes that are often protruding. As the fish loses freshness, the eyes become cloudy, pink, and sunken.
- Bright red or pink gills. Avoid fish with dull-colored gills that are gray, brown, or green. Fresh fish should be free from slime.
- Firm and elastic flesh that springs back when pressed gently with the finger. With time the flesh becomes soft and slips away from the bone.
- Shiny skin, with scales that adhere lightly. Characteristic colors and markings start to fade as soon as a fish leaves the water.
- A clean, pink intestinal cavity.
- A fresh and mild odor.

Fish fillets should have firm and elastic flesh and a fresh-cut appearance with no browning or drying around the edges. Fillet flesh separates if it is left too long in the case. A clean, mild odor is also a must. Fresh fish, or thawed frozen fish, should be kept in the coldest part of the refrigerator and cooked within one or two days.

FLOUR

Refined or processed flours, like white or cake flour, can be stored at room temperature. Purchase only well-sealed, tear-free bags. Either transfer flour from package to a tightly sealed canister or place the whole package itself in a heavy, sealed plastic bag. Store in a cool, dark, dry place for six months, even up to a year under ideal conditions. Try adding a bay leaf to the canister to help ward off insect infestation. Whole-grain flours, on the other hand, because they contain the wheat germ and the outer layer of bran, are far more perishable. Under the same conditions as for refined flour, they will keep well for only about a month. Refrigerated or frozen, whole-wheat flour will keep for up to a year; other whole-grain flours, such as rye and bran, for as little as two months. Check for ''off'' taste to signal that the flour has become stale. If even a trace of mold appears, discard.

FROG'S LEGS

Frog's legs are sometimes available fresh from specialty fish markets. Know your fishmonger and accept only the freshest-appearing and -smelling legs. Highly perishable, frog's legs should be kept in the coldest part of the refrigerator for no more than twenty-four hours.

G

GARBANZOS
See BEANS, DRIED.

GARLIC
Fresh garlic, which may be creamy white or have a purplish red cast, should be plump and firm, with its paperlike covering intact—neither spongy, soft, nor shriveled. Store in a cool, dry, dark place with adequate ventilation, where garlic will keep well for up to a month. Eventually garlic that is held in open-air storage for any length of time will lose much of its pungency. If it does, or if sprouts develop, the garlic is still usable, but it will be somewhat milder, and more may be needed to achieve the same strength of flavor in the dish being prepared. Cut away and discard any green sprouts, which will have a bitter flavor. Refrigeration of garlic is not recommended. However, if fresh garlic must be kept for a long time, it can be peeled and the whole cloves dropped into olive oil and stored in a tightly sealed container in the refrigerator for as long as three months. Garlic can also be frozen when you have a large amount to store. Buy only the freshest heads. Separate the heads into cloves (no need to peel) and place them on a cookie sheet in the freezer until thoroughly frozen. In plastic freezer bags, they will keep indefinitely. To use, simply remove as many as you need and peel while still frozen. The garlic will be quite suitable for cooking. The same recommendations apply to so-called elephant garlic, which is simply a much larger and milder variety of regular garlic.

GELATIN
Gelatins, both flavored and unflavored, are universally available. Purchase at a store with heavy turnover of these products, and be sure packages or envelopes are well sealed and

free from tears. Store on a cool, dry, dark kitchen shelf, where flavored gelatins, such as **Jell-O**, will keep for a year or more and the unflavored kind will last almost indefinitely.

GIBLETS

The giblets of any kind of fowl consist of the gizzard, liver, and heart. Always separate giblets from the bird immediately and cook the same day of purchase. If you buy them separately, look for firm, glossy giblets with good color and fresh odor. Store in the coldest part of the refrigerator.

GINGER POWDER

Unless you plan to bake huge quantities of gingerbread and gingerman cookies, buy ginger powder in the smallest available container. There is no economy in large, bargain-priced containers of herbs and spices. Like all dried spices, ginger loses its punch over a period of time. Keep it with other dried herbs and spices in a cool, dark cupboard or pantry. Do not expose to light and especially not to sources of heat, such as the stove. Keep the container tightly closed at all times. Ginger powder, under these conditions, will stay reasonably potent for up to six months. When the bright gingery-brown color of the powder starts to look dull, the spice is over the hill. A small, self-adhering label indicating date of purchase will help to keep track of shelf life.

GINGER ROOT

This highly pungent root, used commonly in Chinese and Indian cuisines, is now found year-round in most supermarkets. The knobby-looking tuber has light brown skin and moist, fibrous, yellowish green flesh. Look for a large clump of ginger that feels firm, has no withered knobs, and smells fresh. The skin should have a light, uniform color and be free from cuts and deep bruises. Ginger will keep for several weeks in a cool, dark, well-ventilated place or in a plastic bag in the refrigerator. If the smaller knobs become shriveled and dry, they may be cut off and discarded. The main body of the root may still remain quite fresh and usable. Ginger takes well to the freezer, where it will keep for a month or more. Marinated in sherry, it will last for many months in the refrigerator.

GOAT CHEESE
See CHEESE.

GOOSE
Not commonplace, fresh geese are sometimes available, especially from fine butchers in large cities, and require the same care in selection and storage as any poultry (see CHICKEN and TURKEY). Most geese that reach the market, however, have been frozen and are available only around the holiday season. Be sure they are frozen solid with no accumulation of fluid in the package to indicate that the goose was frozen and thawed. Many have an expiration date attached, which will tell you how many more months the goose can remain frozen. Always thaw your goose completely in the refrigerator before cooking.

GOOSEBERRY
This tart relative of the currant is used primarily in jams and cooked desserts. It may be found in limited quantity from April through August, reaching its peak in June and July. Although it comes in various colors, the most common gooseberry is a translucent green with white stripes; it may be covered with a light fuzz. Look for berries that are dry and plump and free from mold. Avoid containers that are seeping juices. Use promptly or store in a plastic bag in the refrigerator for no more than another day or two. Wash just before using.

GRANADILLA
See PASSION FRUIT.

GRAPE
Good domestic grapes are available from June through November, while grapes are imported from Chile and elsewhere during the winter. Regardless of the variety, choose plump, well-colored grapes that are firmly attached to green, pliable stems. Soft or wrinkled grapes or those with bleached areas around the stem are past their prime. Green grapes will be sweetest when yellow green in color. Red varieties are best when rich, red color predominates. Darker varieties should have a deep blue-black color. Grapes will not continue to ripen after they are picked. (The best way to check for sweetness is to taste one.) They are quite perishable and should be refrigerated as soon as possible after purchase. Store unwashed grapes in a plastic bag in the refrigerator, where they will keep for up to five days. Wash gently and serve grapes chilled for best flavor.

GRAPEFRUIT
Grapefruit are available year-round but are at their best from January to June. They come in various sizes and tints and, like all citrus fruit, are picked ripe. Look for firm, glossy fruit with smooth skins, free from blemishes, soft spots, and mold. The most important thing to look for, whether the fruit is white or pink, is a grapefruit that feels heavy for its size and is relatively thin-skinned. The heavy, thin-skinned fruit will be the sweetest and juiciest. Feel the fruit for a smooth texture and avoid if it seems puffy or loose-skinned. Thick-skinned grapefruit may come to a point at the stem end, a feature to be avoided. Skin that has russet or brownish markings or a greenish tint does not indicate poor quality; the fruit is perfectly ripe. Grapefruit will keep at room temperature for up to a week. Store away from heat or direct sun-

light in a well-ventilated room. For longer storage, keep grapefruit in the refrigerator in the covered vegetable crisper, where temperatures are warmer than in the rest of the refrigerator. It will keep there for about ten days to two weeks.

GREAT NORTHERN BEANS
See BEANS, DRIED.

GREEN BEAN
The green bean and its yellow cousin, the **wax bean**, are, except for color, interchangeable, and both are available throughout the year, though at their peak of freshness in the summer. They are also known as **snap beans** or **string beans** (though the inedible "string" has long since been bred out of them). Whether yellow or green, look for bright, clear color, a velvety texture, and especially for a bean that really snaps when bent. A limp or wilting (overage) bean won't snap. Select long, straight, slender pods with small seeds. Beans that have begun to ridge and bulge will be tough. Use promptly or refrigerate for no more than two or three days in a plastic bag. Wash just before using.

GREEN ONION
See SCALLION.

GREEN SQUASH
See SQUASH, SUMMER.

GREENS
With the exception of spinach, all of these leafy green vegetables are cooked rather than used fresh in salads. They should have crisp green leaves. Reject any that display coarse stems, wilted, yellowing leaves, or signs of insect damage. Use promptly or refrigerate in a plastic bag for no more than a day or two. Wash just before using. See also specific kinds

of greens: BEET GREENS, COLLARDS, KALE, MUS-
TARD GREENS, SPINACH, SWISS CHARD, TURNIP
GREENS.

GRITS
See HOMINY.

GROATS
See CEREAL.

GUAVA
This tropical fruit is cultivated in Florida, California, and
Hawaii and is available primarily in the winter months. Varying in both shape and color, the guava is generally oval-
shaped, about the size of a plum, and light green to yellow
in hue. Select firm, unblemished fruit and let ripen at room
temperature away from direct sunlight. When a guava yields
to gentle pressure and emits a fruity aroma, it is ready to eat.
It will keep for a few days in the crisper.

HALF-AND-HALF
See CREAM.

HAM
Various types of ham are available in most markets. Thinly
sliced cooked ham, like other cold cuts, should be well
wrapped, refrigerated, and consumed within two or three
days. Canned hams are usually fully cooked (check label to
be sure) and should be refrigerated until ready to use. An
unopened canned ham will keep for six months or more, but
once opened, the leftovers should be well wrapped and con-

sumed within a week. Discard if even a trace of mold appears. Most ordinary supermarket hams (so-called brine-cured hams) whether whole or half, have also been fully cooked. If you can see it, a brine-cured ham should have firm, pink flesh, but often you may have to rely on the last-day-of-sale date on the label. Depending on that date, you can keep the ham in the refrigerator in its original packaging for up to two weeks. Leftovers should be tightly wrapped and consumed within a week.

So-called country, or dry-cured hams, of which the **Smithfield** is perhaps the best known, are usually smoked and aged for long periods of time. They do not need refrigeration before they are cut and will keep in a cool, airy place for a year or more. Once cooked (country ham requires cooking), they will keep in the refrigerator up to six weeks. Other dry-cured hams like **Westphalian** and **prosciutto** are sliced paper thin and eaten raw. They should be wrapped well, refrigerated, and consumed within three or four days. So-called fresh ham is not really ham at all but rather a leg of pork that has not been cured in any way.

HAMBURGER
See BEEF.

HAZELNUT (FILBERT)
Always available, hazelnuts are usually sold in the shell. They should be clean and free from cracks and other surface blemishes. If the shell rattles when shaken, the kernel is likely to be dried out. Stored in a tightly sealed canister on a cool, dry, dark shelf, they will keep for about a month, in the refrigerator for three or four months. In the freezer, they will last for a year or more. See also NUTS.

HEART
See VARIETY MEATS.

HERBS AND SPICES

The distinction between an herb and a spice is somewhat technical, and opinions vary on just what it is. One authority states that herbs grow in temperate climates, spices in tropical, with the exception of bay, which grows in either. In terms of selecting and storing them, however, it makes little difference. One knows almost instinctively, for example, that parsley and tarragon are herbs and pepper and nutmeg are spices.

Fresh herbs, in general, should look fresh: have sprightly green leaves, be free from yellowing, wilting, and insect damage, and have an appealing aroma. They should be rinsed thoroughly and patted dry with a paper towel. Sealed in a plastic bag, they will keep for about a week in the refrigerator. Basil is an exception: it abhors cold and should be kept in a glass of water like flowers in a vase. Most fresh herbs may also be chopped, dried thoroughly, and kept in small plastic bags in the freezer for six months or more.

Many dried herbs and spices come in both whole and ground form. The whole will last considerably longer than the ground, for up to a year as opposed to six months. Glass and tin containers are preferred over cellophane and plastic, which can let in air and hasten deterioration of the product. Purchase dried herbs and spices in the smallest available quantities, and keep tightly sealed in a cool, dark cabinet or pantry. Do not expose to light and especially not to sources of heat, such as a stove. Fading color and/or aroma are sure signs that the spice or herb is over the hill. A small, self-adhering label indicating date of purchase will help to keep track of shelf life.

See also specific herbs and spices.

HOMINY

Hominy consists of dried kernels of corn from which the germ has been removed. When hominy is ground, it is referred to as hominy **grits**. To keep out insects, store hominy or grits in a tightly sealed, nonmetallic canister or seal the package itself in a heavy plastic bag. If properly stored in a cool, dark, dry cabinet, hominy will keep for up to a year.

HONEY

Select a tightly sealed jar and store at room temperature on a dry, dark kitchen shelf. Always reseal the jar promptly and tightly, as honey will absorb moisture and food odors if exposed too long to the air. Wipe thoroughly around the lid after each use to remove any residue that might attract insects. Honey will keep for up to a year. Do not refrigerate honey or it will soon crystallize. Some crystallization may occur in time even at room temperature; in that event, simply immerse the honey jar in a pan of warm (not hot) water until the crystals dissolve.

HONEYDEW

Honeydew melons may be found most of the year in some stores, but they are at their peak from June through October, with the best coming to market in late summer. They should feel heavy for their size. The flesh of the honeydew is green, but the rind should have a creamy or buttery color; green would indicate that the melon was picked prematurely, in which case it will not ripen further. The honeydew should also have a slightly velvety rather than fully smooth texture. The blossom end (opposite the stem end where the melon was picked from the vine) should give slightly to gentle pressure. The ripening fruit will exude a sweet, melony aroma. Avoid honeydews with broken rind, soft spots, or large discolored areas. If the melon is not fully ripe, leave it at room temperature, away from direct sunlight, for several days. It can then be refrigerated in a plastic bag for up to a week more.

HORSERADISH

Horseradish is a fleshy, white cylindrical root that may be found fresh in some retail outlets throughout the year. A firm, well-formed root with a pungent odor is desirable. Wrapped airtight in plastic and refrigerated, horseradish will keep for up to two months.

HOT DOG

Look for well-sealed hot dogs, or **frankfurters**, with no tear or puncture in their plastic container. Keep in the refrigerator, where, unopened, they will store safely up to the "sell by" date on the package. Once opened, continue to refrigerate and use up hot dogs within a week. Discard if even a trace of mold appears.

HUBBARD SQUASH

This large and colorful winter squash is available during the fall and winter. Round and thick-necked, the Hubbard may be green, blue, or reddish orange. The bumpy rind should be firm and hard, and the squash should have a heavy feel for its size, indicating that it is moist inside. Look for a dull rather than shiny surface and a rind free from bruises, gouges, and soft or sunken spots. Hubbard squash will keep for a week or so at normal room temperatures. In a cool, airy place, away from direct sunlight, with temperatures around 50°F, it will keep for one or more months. In hot weather, refrigerate for up to two weeks.

HUCKLEBERRY

Huckleberries grow on shrubs in the wild and are rarely sold commercially. The best way to enjoy them fresh in the summer is to pick your own. More tart than a blueberry, which it resembles, the huckleberry also has larger seeds and is more often used in cooking. Select fruit of good, deep blue-black color that is firm and free from mold and bruises. Keep unwashed in the refrigerator in a covered glass or plastic container for from one to two weeks.

I

ICE CREAM
Ice cream and **sherbet** should always be purchased from a retail outlet with high turnover of these products. Choose a carton that is very firm and shows no signs of having defrosted. Avoid any carton that feels the least bit mushy or one that has stains indicating that some of the contents have melted. Make ice cream one of your last purchases at the market and get it home into the freezer with all due speed. Ice cream, unopened, will keep for up to two months at 0°F, but because of the temperature fluctuations in most frost-free freezers, it is best consumed within one week of purchase. Once opened, seal the whole carton inside a heavy plastic bag to prevent freezer burn and absorption of odors.

ICEBERG LETTUCE
See LETTUCE, ICEBERG.

ITALIAN PARSLEY
See PARSLEY.

J

JALAPEÑO PEPPER
See PEPPER (HOT).

JAM
Select a tightly sealed jar at the market and store for up to a year, unopened, on a cool, dry, dark kitchen shelf. Once opened, the jam will keep for about a month at room temperature, but refrigeration is recommended unless you expect to use up the jam very quickly. If jam is left on the shelf, always wipe clean around the lid so that no trace is left to attract insects. Refrigerated, jam will keep for about six months. If mold forms on the surface, remove a thin layer that contains the mold and use the rest of the jam promptly.

JELL-O
See GELATIN.

JELLY
Select a tightly sealed jar at the market and store for up to a year, unopened, on a cool, dry, dark kitchen shelf. Once opened, the jelly will keep for about a month at room temperature, but refrigeration is recommended unless you expect to use up the jelly very quickly. If jelly is left on the shelf, always wipe clean around the lid so that no trace is left to attract insects. Refrigerated, jelly will keep for about six months. If mold forms on the surface, remove a thin layer that contains the mold and use the rest of the jelly promptly.

JERUSALEM ARTICHOKE
Often called **sunchoke**, the Jerusalem artichoke is a brown root vegetable whose nutty flavor is often compared with that of the more familiar globe artichoke. It is commonly available from October to April but may be found in some places

throughout the year. The vegetable has a gnarled appearance that has been likened to a cross between a potato and ginger root. Look for firm, hard, clean tubers with no soft spots or sprouting. Store in a plastic bag in the refrigerator for up to two weeks.

JICAMA
This root vegetable grows in many tropical areas of the world and is often used in Mexican and Chinese cooking. Like a potato, it is characterized by brown outer skin and firm, white flesh. The taste of raw jicama is often compared with that of water chestnuts. Select firm, unbruised jicamas. The smaller ones (jicamas range from one to six pounds) are considered the more desirable. Refrigerate for up to two weeks.

KALE
Related to the cabbage, kale is available year-round. Its large, curly leaves may be dark green or even bluish in tone. Choose fresh, young, and well-colored leaves. Avoid any with coarse stems or wilted, yellowing foliage. Keep in the refrigerator in a sealed plastic bag and use promptly, within a day or two at most. Wash just before using.

KETCHUP
Unopened, ketchup, or **catsup**, as it is also known, will keep for up to a year on a kitchen shelf away from sources of light and heat. Once opened, ketchup should be refrigerated. It will keep there, tightly sealed, for up to six months.

KIDNEY
See VARIETY MEATS.

KIDNEY BEANS
See BEANS, DRIED.

KIELBASA
See SAUSAGE.

KIWIFRUIT
Because kiwifruit is grown in both California and New Zealand, in opposite hemispheres of the world, it is available year-round at the market. The California kiwifruit is harvested in October and available into May. On the outside, a kiwifruit is fuzzy and brown; inside, it's a brilliant emerald green. Kiwifruit should be plump, egg-shaped, and free from wrinkles, cuts, and bruises. When ripe, the skin should give slightly to gentle finger pressure. If the kiwifruit are too hard, simply leave them at room temperature, away from direct sunlight, for a few days until they reach the right degree of softness, then store them in your refrigerator's egg compartment, where they will keep for up to two weeks. Hard kiwifruit will also ripen in the refrigerator over a period of several weeks. To ripen kiwifruit quickly, place in a plastic bag with an ethylene-gas-producing fruit such as a banana or pear. You should have fully ripened kiwifruit in twenty-four hours. Because of their susceptibility to ethylene, it is best to store kiwifruit apart from other fruit in the refrigerator.

KNOB CELERY
See CELERY ROOT.

KNOCKWURST
See SAUSAGE.

KOHLRABI

A member of the cabbage family, kohlrabi means "cabbage turnip" (an apt description) in German. At its peak in the summer, kohlrabi is also available throughout the year. Its globular bulb has a delicate turniplike taste; its tops can be used like any other fresh greens. Look for firm, light green bulbs with no soft spots or indentations and for nonyellowing, unwilted greens. (Sometimes the vegetable is sold without the greens.) Bulbs larger than about two inches in diameter may be tough and bitter. Store in a plastic bag in the refrigerator for up to four days and cut off the stems just before using.

KUMQUAT

Available from December to May, this citruslike fruit may be found in limited supply, especially in urban areas with large Oriental populations. Kumquats look like miniature oranges. They should be firm, of good uniform color, and heavy for their size. Those tinged with green will be unripe and overly tart. Ripe kumquats will keep for several weeks in the refrigerator.

LAMB

In general, the younger the lamb at slaughter, the more tender the meat. The youngest are labeled "genuine Spring lamb," and somewhat older ones just plain "Spring lamb." The younger lamb will also have a paler pink color; the older the animal, the darker the meat tends to become. Always check for an expiration date on the label and look for pink, finely textured lamb with as little fat as possible. Eschew lamb in a torn package or one with an accumulation of blood in it;

meat in the latter may have been frozen and thawed or may simply have been sitting too long in its prepackaged tray. White fat and reddish, porous bones are also desirable. After the lamb reaches a year, it is called **mutton**, a meat rarely seen in American markets. Store lamb in its original wrapping in the coldest part of the refrigerator if you plan to use it the day of purchase or the next. If it is to be stored longer, rewrap loosely in plastic or foil to allow air to circulate about the meat. Be careful lest drippings that might contain harmful bacteria fall on other foods or refrigerator shelves. Larger roast cuts and chops will keep for up to four days, but ground lamb or stew meat should be stored no more than two days.

LAMB'S LETTUCE

Also known as **mâche, field salad**, and **corn salad**, this salad green has a sweet, slightly peppery taste. It is available year-round, though not in every supermarket. The dark green, almost bluish, rounded leaves should be free from wilting and yellowing. Very perishable, lamb's lettuce should be refrigerated in a plastic bag as soon as possible and used within a day of purchase. Wash just before using.

LARD

Like vegetable shortening, lard (which is rendered and clarified pork fat), unless otherwise stated on the label, may be kept at room temperature on a cool, dry shelf for up to a year.

LEEK

A member of the onion family and an essential ingredient of vichyssoise, leeks are called the poor man's asparagus in Europe. They are known as the mildest of the onions. They are available year-round but are at their best in winter and early spring. Leeks are always described as looking like giant scallions, but while scallions may have rounded bulbs, the bulb of the leek is straight-sided and cylindrical. Look for well-blanched bunches, with the white coloring extending two to three inches from the base of the bulb. Small or medium-size leeks will be the best-tasting. Eschew bunches that are excessively gritty, though any leeks will have to be washed very thoroughly to rid them of sand. The leaves should be crisp and fresh-looking, the stalks firm yet pliable. Refrigerate in a sealed plastic bag for up to a week.

LEMON
Lemons are available year-round. As with all citrus, look for firm, glossy fruit with smooth skins, free from blemishes, soft spots, and mold. Minor discoloration or a greenish cast do not indicate poor quality. Also, as with other citrus fruit, select lemons that are thin-skinned and feel heavy for their size. These will be the juiciest. Avoid fruit with loose or spongy skin. Since it's generally true that the smaller the lemon, the thinner the skin, selecting the largest (and more expensive) lemons may not give you the juiciest fruit. Speaking of juice, a lemon will yield more fluid if firmly rolled around on a countertop under the palm of the hand before squeezing it. Lemons will keep at room temperature for up to a week. Store away from heat or direct sunlight in a well-ventilated room. For longer storage, place lemons in a sealed plastic bag and keep in the covered vegetable crisper of the refrigerator, where they will keep for two to three weeks.

LENTILS
See BEANS, DRIED.

LETTUCE
Apart from **iceberg** (see below), all lettuces can be selected and stored in much the same manner. Popular varieties include **Boston**, or **butterhead**; **Bibb**, or **limestone**; **romaine**, sometimes known as **cos**; and **leaf**, or **salad bowl** (leaf let-

tuce may be either green or red-tipped). In all cases, select fresh-looking, crisp, bright-colored heads or bunches. Avoid wilted or browning leaves or a generally tired appearance. Place unwashed lettuce in a sealed plastic bag and store in the refrigerator, where it will keep for up to a week, depending on the variety. The firmer romaine, for example, is likely to keep a bit longer than the softer leaf lettuce. When ready to use, separate the leaves and wash thoroughly under cold, running water. Spin dry or dry with paper towels, but do dry as completely as possible, because excessive moisture promotes wilting and spoilage in lettuce. It also makes it difficult for salad dressing to adhere to the leaves. Wrap unused leaves in paper toweling, seal in a plastic bag, and keep for up to another week in the refrigerator. (Although these leaves may stay reasonably crisp, it should be noted that they lose considerable nutritive value.) There is little hope for lettuce leaves once they have wilted, but if desperate, try placing them in the freezer for no more than a minute or two.

LETTUCE, ICEBERG
Ubiquitous iceberg lettuce requires somewhat special handling. Heads should be crisp and clean, never wilted or flabby. Heads should also be free from rusty blotches (though a little browning around the core is normal). The head should feel light in weight in comparison to its size and should feel firm but still give slightly when gently squeezed. Avoid heads with very pale or washed-out color. Though often faulted for its lack of flavor and nutritive value, iceberg does keep longer than other lettuces in the refrigerator. Store unwashed in a sealed plastic bag until ready to use; it will keep for up to two weeks. Unwrapped lettuce should never be stored near ethylene-producing fruits such as apples, bananas, and pears, since ethylene hastens decay in lettuce.

To core iceberg, strike the head firmly, core side down, on a countertop and lift or twist out the core. You may also core with a knife, but be sure to use stainless steel since carbon steel will discolor lettuce. To rinse, place the head, core side up, under forcefully running cold water. Never submerge lettuce completely because it will absorb too much moisture, which may damage the head and make it difficult to dry thoroughly. To dry, place head, core side down, in a colander and allow lettuce to drain thoroughly; or use a spin dryer to expedite the drying process. Excess water can cause browning and hasten spoilage. Again, store unused lettuce in a sealed plastic bag, in the refrigerator, where it will keep for several more days.

LIMA BEAN

Fresh lima beans are a rarity in supermarkets but may be found in some areas during the summer months. The large pods should be firm, crisp, of good green color and velvety texture. The kidney-shaped inner bean may be large (called **Fordhooks**, or **butter beans**) or small (called **baby limas**) and should also be of good green color. *Eating raw lima beans is not recommended; they may induce an allergic reaction.* Use promptly or refrigerate for no more than a day or two in a plastic bag.

LIME

Like all citrus fruit, limes should be firm and glossy with smooth skins, free from blemishes, soft spots, and mold. Look for deep green skins. Unless they are Key limes, fruit with yellowish skins are probably past their prime. (Key limes, the source of the famous pie that bears their name, are naturally yellow but rarely seen outside of Florida.) Like other citrus fruit, limes should feel heavy for their size, indicating more juiciness. A good way to get the most juice out of a lime: roll it about firmly on the countertop with the palm of your hand before squeezing. More juice will also flow if the lime is removed from the refrigerator about an hour before you plan to use it. Available year-round, limes are at their peak in the summer. Limes may be kept out of sunlight at room temperature for up to a week but are best stored in a sealed plastic bag in the refrigerator, where they will keep for three or four weeks or longer. After prolonged refrigeration, limes may show signs of pitting and refrigerator burn.

LINGUINE

Linguine, like most pastas, is nothing more than flour and water. There is little one can do to detect freshness in a package of dried linguine other than to be sure that the package has not been violated and that the place of purchase is one with high turnover of this product. Unopened, dried linguine will keep on a kitchen shelf for several months without undue deterioration. For longer storage, transfer linguine to a tightly sealed glass or plastic container and keep in a dark, dry cabinet for up to a year. Fresh linguine is much more perishable; be sure that it was indeed made fresh very recently. Keep refrigerated and use within a day or two.

LITCHI
See LYCHEE.

LIVER

Liver is commonly available in supermarkets. Calf's liver is usually the more tender, beef somewhat tougher and stronger of flavor. Look for light yet richly colored calf's liver of pale reddish brown, a shiny appearance, and a lack of odor. Beef, pork, chicken, and lamb liver will be a darker red. Keep liver in the coldest part of the refrigerator and use the day of purchase or next at the latest. It is quite perishable. Wrap loosely so that air may circulate about the liver.

LOBSTER

Like all shellfish, lobsters are extremely perishable. You may find them year-round, but they are at their best in the warmer months. Purchase at a market that has a heavy turnover of lobsters. If you trap them yourself, know the waters to be sure they are not polluted. Lobsters should be bought literally live and kicking. Size has little to do with quality. One-clawed lobsters are perfectly fine for eating and usually a good buy. Very active lobsters, stored in seaweed, may keep for a couple of days in the refrigerator but are best consumed on the day of purchase. They must still be alive when you cook them. Precooked lobsters (always to be cooked on day of purchase) should be bright red and fresh-smelling; if their tails curl back when pulled, you have assurance that they were cooked live.

LOGANBERRY

The loganberry looks like a red blackberry and is thought to be a hybrid between a blackberry and a raspberry. Loganberries are at their peak from June until August. They should be purchased at the peak of ripeness and consumed as soon as possible. Examine loganberries carefully. They should have a deep, glossy red color. Look for berries that are dry and plump and well formed. Avoid those that still have green caps attached, as that indicates they were picked too early. There should be no sign of mold, rot, and bruising or of seeping juices on the container. If you can't eat them the same day, gently pick over the berries, discarding any that are too soft or moldy, and store the remainder, unwashed, for no more than another day or two in the refrigerator. Spread the berries in a single layer on a paper towel and cover loosely with plastic wrap. Wash, again gently, just before using.

LOQUAT

Chinese in origin, the loquat is cultivated in California and Florida. Hardly a common fruit, it may be found in some specialty outlets in the spring. Physically, the loquat resembles an apricot, but its tart flavor has been compared with that of apples, pears, and cherries. Look for unblemished fruit that yields to gentle pressure, and consume promptly or refrigerate in a plastic bag for a day or two.

LYCHEE

Sometimes spelled **litchi**, this Oriental fruit is rarely found fresh outside of large Asian-urban neighborhoods. It has a brief spring season. About the size of a golf ball, the lychee has a pebbly reddish skin that peels easily to reveal juicy white flesh and a brown pit. Look for firm, unblemished fruit (some browning is normal) that has a heavy feel for its size. Lychees will keep for a week or more in the refrigerator. Dried lychees, called lychee nuts, will keep for several months.

M

MACADAMIA

This highly prized and costly nut is virtually always sold in roasted/salted form and is available year-round. Look for a tightly sealed jar and plump, crisp nuts. Keep unopened on a cool, dry, dark shelf for up to a year, but once opened, store macadamias in a tightly sealed container in the refrigerator, where they will keep up to six months. See also NUTS.

MACARONI

Macaroni, like most pastas, is nothing more than flour and water. There is little one can do to detect freshness in a package of dried macaroni other than to be sure that the package has not been violated and that the place of purchase is one with high turnover of this product. Unopened, dried macaroni will keep on a kitchen shelf for several months without undue deterioration. For longer storage, transfer macaroni to a tightly sealed glass or plastic container and keep in a dark, dry cabinet for up to a year. Fresh macaroni is much more perishable; be sure that it was indeed made fresh very recently. Keep refrigerated and use within a day or two.

MÂCHE

See LAMB'S LETTUCE.

MALANGA

A large, brown, potatolike tuber, the malanga is available year-round, especially in urban areas with large Hispanic populations. Its flesh is more yam- than potato-colored and more starchy in taste and texture than that of the potato. Look for firm malangas, free from cracks and bruises. Store at room temperature for several days, in the refrigerator for about a week.

MANDARIN ORANGE

The mandarin orange looks like a small tangerine and, like that fruit, should have a bright, glossy skin, free from blemishes, soft spots, and mold. The orange color is somewhat lighter than that of the tangerine, and the fruit has a mild, sweet flavor and few seeds. Look for mandarins that feel heavy for their size, which indicates juiciness. The skin fits somewhat tighter than that of the tangerine, but the mandarin can also be easily peeled and segmented. Mandarins are in season from November through May. Like all oranges, they will keep well for a week or so at room temperature, away from heat and direct sunlight. For longer storage, up to several weeks, place in a sealed plastic bag in the refrigerator.

MANGO

This round or oval-shaped tropical fruit is usually about the size of a large pear, though there are much smaller and much bigger varieties. Its sweet flavor has been compared with that of ripe peaches and apricots. Imported throughout the year, mangoes are at their peak from May to August. The basic skin color is green with yellowish to reddish areas. The red and yellow areas increase as the mango ripens. Look for fruit that is firm, smooth, plump, and fragrant. Some black spotting is normal as the mango ripens, but soft or bruised spots should be avoided. Also to be avoided: grayish skin discoloration and pitting. Keep mangoes at room temperature until they are quite soft, then consume promptly. Refrigeration is not recommended, but if necessary, mangoes will keep there for a day or two after they ripen.

MANIOC
See YUCCA.

MAPLE SYRUP

A tightly sealed jar or tin of maple syrup will keep, unopened, on the kitchen shelf for a year or more. Once opened, it should be refrigerated. Bring to room temperature before using to allow the syrup to pour smoothly. It will keep for up to a year in the refrigerator. If mold forms on the surface, skim it off, boil the remaining syrup, decant into a sterilized canning jar, return to the refrigerator when cool, and use promptly.

MARGARINE
See BUTTER.

MARJORAM
A sweet and milder cousin of oregano, fresh marjoram may be found year-round in a limited number of retail outlets. Not so green as some other herbs, marjoram should still be free from yellowing and wilting. Rinse thoroughly and pat dry with a paper towel. Kept sealed in a plastic bag in the refrigerator, marjoram should stay fresh for about a week. For longer storage, up to six months or more, seal chopped and thoroughly dried marjoram leaves in a small plastic bag and freeze. Dried marjoram leaves should be kept with other dried herbs and spices in a cool, dark cupboard or pantry. Do not expose to light and especially not to sources of heat, such as a stove. Keep the container tightly closed at all times. Dried marjoram, under these conditions, should retain some potency for up to a year. When its color becomes pale and dull, the herb is probably over the hill. A good sniff for the characteristic smell of marjoram is also a useful check on its freshness. A small, self-adhering label indicating date of purchase will help to keep track of shelf life.

MARMALADE
Select a tightly sealed jar at the market and store for up to a year, unopened, on a cool, dry, dark kitchen shelf. Once opened, marmalade will keep for about a month at room temperature, but refrigeration is recommended unless you expect to use up the marmalade very quickly. If marmalade is left on the shelf, always wipe clean around the lid so that no trace is left to attract insects. Refrigerated, marmalade will keep for about six months. If mold forms on the surface, remove a thin layer that contains the mold and use the rest of the marmalade fairly promptly.

MAYONNAISE

Unopened, mayonnaise and imitation mayonnaise will keep for up to a year on a kitchen shelf away from sources of light and heat. Always heed the "sell by" date on the label. Once opened, mayonnaise should be refrigerated and returned promptly to the refrigerator after each use. Tightly sealed, it will keep there for up to six months. Leftover homemade mayonnaise should also be refrigerated but used within a day or two.

MELON

Melons of some kinds are available throughout the year, but the best come to market during the summer and early fall. Look for melons of characteristic color for their type. They should feel heavy for their size and be free from mold, gouges, soft spots, and discoloration. Most will exude a distinctive melony aroma as they ripen and will yield to slight pressure at the blossom end (opposite the stem end where the melon was attached to the vine). Melons will continue to ripen for a few days at room temperature, away from direct sunlight, and should then be refrigerated in a plastic bag, where they will keep for another week or so. See also specific types of melon: CANTALOUPE, CASABA, CRENSHAW, HONEYDEW, WATERMELON.

MILK

It is sometimes assumed that milk must be used by the "sell by" date on the carton, but in fact, if refrigerated at temperatures between 33° and 40°F, milk will keep for up to a week beyond the sell date. Milk is certainly perishable, however, and should always be kept cold. Be sure the carton is well and evenly chilled when you purchase it and that it has no surface stains or leaks. Pick it up at the end of your shopping trip and get it home to the refrigerator with all due speed. Some shoppers prefer to transport milk and other perishables home in a cooler. When pouring milk, use only the amount required and return the carton promptly to the refrigerator rather than leaving it on the table while you eat. Leftover milk from a meal or snack should never be returned to its carton of origin. **Buttermilk** and **cream** (including **half-and-half**) require similar handling and storage. Cream in particular should be kept in the very coldest part of the refrigerator. Buttermilk will keep longer than milk or cream, up to two weeks.

MINT

There are many varieties of mint, **spearmint** and **peppermint** being the most common, some of which may be found year-round in some retail outlets. The leaves should be fresh-appearing and free from yellowing and wilting. Rinse thoroughly and pat dry with a paper towel. Kept sealed in a plastic bag in the refrigerator, mint should stay fresh for about a week. For longer storage, up to six months or more, seal chopped and thoroughly dried mint leaves in a small plastic bag and freeze. Dried mint leaves should be kept with other dried herbs and spices in a cool, dark cupboard or pantry. Do not expose to light and especially not to sources of heat, such as a stove. Keep the container tightly closed at all times. Dried mint, under these conditions, should retain some potency for up to a year. When its color becomes pale and dull, the herb is probably over the hill. A good sniff for the characteristic smell of mint is also a useful check on its freshness. A small, self-adhering label indicating date of purchase will help to keep track of shelf life.

MIRLITON
See CHAYOTE.

MOLASSES

Whether light, dark, or blackstrap, molasses will keep, unopened, for a year or more on a cool, dry, dark kitchen shelf. Once opened, always be sure to wipe thoroughly around the cap so that no residue is left to attract insects. The opened jar of molasses may be kept on that shelf at room temperature for up to another year.

MOZZARELLA

See CHEESE.

MUFFIN

See BREAD.

MULBERRY

Mulberries are not sold commercially. The best way to enjoy them fresh in the summer is to pick them off the tree, which is both cultivated and grows wild in many parts of the United States. They may be black, red, or white and are shaped like a blackberry. Look for firm fruit of good color, free from insect or bird damage. The fragile berry should be handled gently and kept for no more than a day or two in a plastic bag in the refrigerator. Wash just before using.

MURCOTT

See TANGERINE.

MUSHROOM

Mushrooms range in color from white to cream to brown. They are available all year, primarily in domesticated varieties but also, in specialty markets and gourmet sections of supermarkets, in some wild varieties (**cepes, shiitake, chanterelle**, and others). Be wary of extremely white, clean mushrooms; read the label carefully, for they may have been treated with bleaching chemicals. Avoid excessively dirty mushrooms (some dirt is to be expected), and look for caps that are firm, plump, dry, and free from mold or discolored patches. If the gills beneath the cap have darkened and spread like the spokes of an umbrella, the mushroom is old but may still be pungent and suitable for cooking. Mushrooms that feel slimy should be discarded. Let any that feel merely damp dry out at room temperature, but do not wash before refrigerating. Mushrooms keep best in a brown paper bag with a damp paper towel placed over them. They should keep fresh this way for four or five days. Do not wrap in plastic, which makes mushrooms turn slimy. Clean with a damp paper towel just before using. Presliced mushrooms should be refrigerated and used as soon as possible, preferably within twenty-four hours. Dried mushrooms should be kept in a cool, dry place in a tightly sealed container, where they may last for many months. See also TRUFFLE.

MUSSEL
Like all shellfish, mussels are extremely perishable. You can buy them year-round, but they are generally better during the colder months. Purchase mussels at a market that has a heavy turnover of shellfish. If you gather them yourself, know the waters to be sure they are not polluted. Mussels should be bought live. You can tell they're alive if the shells are tightly closed or snap shut when touched. (Conversely, mussels open when they're cooked; those that remain closed should be discarded.) Avoid mussels with broken shells or off odor as well as those that feel unusually heavy (the latter may be weighted with sand). Refrigerate mussels and consume within twenty-four hours of purchase. If you must buy shucked mussels, be sure of your fishmonger and use the same day.

MUSTARD
Prepared mustard, unopened, will keep for up to a year on a kitchen shelf away from sources of light and heat. Once

opened, mustard should be refrigerated. It will keep there, tightly sealed, for six months or even longer, though some varieties may lose some of their zest after prolonged storage. Dried mustard, like other dried herbs and spices, should be kept in a tightly sealed container in a cool, dark, dry place. It will retain pungency for up to a year.

MUTTON
See LAMB.

NAPPA
See CHINESE CABBAGE.

NAVY BEANS
See BEANS, DRIED.

NECTARINE
The nectarine is generally considered to be a fruit unto itself, not merely a fuzzless peach or a peach-plum hybrid. Nectarines are at their best in summer, from June through August. It is not true that a reddish blush indicates an especially fresh or sweet nectarine; the blush only indicates the variety, not the ripeness of the fruit. The background, or "ground," color should be a rich, creamy golden yellow, free from bruises, blemishes, and soft spots. Fruit that is greenish in color, especially small, or excessively hard will most likely fail to ripen properly. A nectarine that yields slightly to palm pressure along its "seam" and that emits a ripe aroma is ready to eat. For further ripening, place nectarines in a loosely closed paper bag or ripening bowl for two or three days, checking them regularly. Once refrigerated, they will

not continue to ripen but will keep well in a plastic bag for several days.

NOODLES
See EGG NOODLES.

NOPALES
Also known as **cactus leaves**, which they are, nopales resemble green beans in taste. Select firm, fresh-looking leaves, noting that the smaller nopales will be the more tender. Cactus barbs are usually removed before shipping, but best be wary in handling the leaves. Not a common item of produce, they may be found in limited supply, especially in the Southwest. Refrigerate in a plastic bag and use within a couple of days.

NUTMEG
A nutmeg is the kernel, or seed, of a tropical fruit and is sold in both whole and ground form. Store with other dried herbs and spices in a cool, dark cupboard or pantry. Do not expose to light and especially not to sources of heat, such as a stove. Keep the container tightly closed at all times. Ground nutmeg may retain its potency for up to six months, the whole nutmegs for a year or more. Fading color and aroma are sure signs that the spice is over the hill. A small, self-adhering label indicating date of purchase will help to keep track of shelf life.

NUTS
Look for unshelled nuts that feel heavy for their size and are free from mold, cracks, and other surface damage. If you shake a shell and it makes a rattling sound, the kernel is probably dry and stale. Unshelled nuts will keep in an open bowl away from direct sun and heat for about a month. For longer storage, refrigerate them in a tightly sealed container

for up to six months. Shelled nuts are more susceptible to spoilage. They should be plump and crisp. In an unopened can or jar, they will keep for up to a year on that kitchen shelf, but once opened they should be consumed promptly. Leftovers, resealed, will keep for about a week at room temperature. For longer storage—four to six months—keep shelled nuts in a tightly sealed container or plastic bag in the refrigerator. They will keep even longer—a year or more— in the freezer. *Always discard any nuts with signs of mold, which may produce something called aflatoxins, carcinogens that have been linked to liver cancer.* The U.S. Food and Drug Administration (FDA) is responsible for monitoring the levels of such molds in nuts. See also specific names of nuts: CASHEW, MACADAMIA, BRAZIL, and so on.

OCTOPUS
See SQUID.

OIL, COOKING
Purchase all oils in markets with fast product turnover. Most **vegetable oils**, including **corn**, **peanut**, **sunflower**, and **safflower**, will keep for up to a year, unopened, in a cool, dark kitchen cabinet. Once opened, close container tightly after each use: oil will keep for up to six months in that cool, dark place. **Olive oil** keeps for about three to four months and **walnut** and **sesame** oil for two. Refrigeration may prolong storage life, especially in hot weather, though it tends to cloud the oil and, some experts contend, hasten its deterioration. Cloudiness will dissipate as the oil returns to room temperature.

OKRA

This pod vegetable, a relative of the cotton plant, is available year-round, especially in the South, where it is commonly used in gumbos and other regional dishes. Okra is sometimes called gumbo for this reason. Look for good green color, for pods that snap easily or puncture when slightly pressed, for a velvety texture, and ideally for pods of no more than 2½ inches in length. A limp or wilted appearance and brown streaks are to be avoided. Fresh okra will keep at its best for three or four days in a plastic bag in the refrigerator. Wash just before using.

OLIVE

Unopened, a tightly sealed jar or can of olives will keep almost indefinitely on a cool, dry, dark kitchen shelf. Once opened, transfer the olives and their liquid (if canned) to a glass container, seal tightly, and refrigerate. Pimiento-stuffed olives will keep for about a month, unpitted olives for several months. A whitish scum on the olives is merely a salty condensation that should be rinsed off before consuming.

OLIVE OIL
See OIL, COOKING.

ONION

Most varieties of onion (**red**, **Spanish**, **white**, **yellow**, **pickling**, **pearl**, **Bermuda**) are available throughout the year. Some of the more prized, sweeter varieties such as **Vidalia**, **Walla Walla**, and **Maui** have shorter spring and summer seasons. Regardless of color or variety, onions should have dry, shiny, paper skins. Avoid at all costs any onions with wet, soggy necks or soft, spongy bulbs, which indicate decay, or with signs of sprouting. Black spots may also signal disease and decay. Look for onions that are clean, firm, and feel heavy in the hand. The skins should be dry, smooth, and crackly. Greenish patches on the skin indicate improper storage; these onions are likely to be bitter and should be avoided. Store all onions in a dark, dry, cool, well-ventilated place. If you use a kitchen cabinet, select one that is not adjacent to stove, steam pipe, dishwasher, or other heat-producing instrument. Do not store onions near potatoes; the chemical interaction of the two vegetables may curtail the shelf life of both. Onions will keep for three to four weeks under ideal conditions, less than that if the air is warm and humid.

ORANGE

Oranges are available year-round. They should be firm and heavy with a fine textured skin. Fruit that feels heavy for its size is desirable, because it indicates that the orange is particularly juicy. Look for smooth, glossy skins, free from breaks and soft spots. Minor skin blemishes and brown mottling do not indicate a problem within. Of course, avoid fruit that is deeply bruised or gouged or moldy. Skin color has little to do with quality or freshness of the orange. Orange groves are closely inspected, and the fruit may not be picked until it reaches an acceptable level of ripeness. Oranges ripen fully on the tree and do not continue to ripen after they are picked. The fruit is fully ripe even though it may have a greenish tinge. Through a curious but natural process called "regreening," oranges may revert from orange to green in color, but this has no effect on their ripeness. Oranges will keep at room temperature for about a week to ten days. Store them away from heat or direct sunlight in a well-ventilated room. For longer storage, keep oranges in the refrigerator in the covered vegetable crisper, where temperatures are warmer than the rest of the refrigerator. They will keep there for two to three weeks.

There are many varieties of orange, including the popular **Valencia** and **navel**, all of which can be handled in the same manner where freshness is concerned. The **Seville** or bitter orange is something else. Though it looks just like a regular orange, it is indeed bitter-tasting and is used primarily for making marmalade. See also TEMPLE ORANGE.

ORANGE JUICE
Freshly squeezed orange juice should be kept in the refrigerator in a tightly sealed glass container with as little air space at the top as possible. It will keep for up to a week, though it will begin to lose some flavor and vitamin C within days. Heed "sell by" dates on store-bought juice, keep refrigerated, and use within two weeks after opening.

OREGANO
Fresh oregano is found throughout the year in an increasing number of retail outlets. This popular herb is not so green as some other fresh herbs but should be free from yellowing and wilting. Rinse thoroughly and pat dry with a paper towel. Kept sealed in a plastic bag in the refrigerator, oregano should stay fresh for about a week. For longer storage, up to six months or more, seal chopped and thoroughly dried oregano leaves in a small plastic bag and freeze. Dried oregano leaves should be kept with other dried herbs and spices in a cool, dark cupboard or pantry. Do not expose to light and especially not to sources of heat, such as a stove. Keep the container tightly closed at all times. Dried oregano, under these conditions, should retain some potency for up to a year. When its color becomes pale and dull, the herb is probably over the hill. A good sniff for the characteristic smell of oregano is also a useful check on its freshness. A small, self-adhering label indicating date of purchase will help to keep track of shelf life.

ORGAN MEATS
See VARIETY MEATS.

OYSTER

Like all shellfish, oysters are extremely perishable. You may find them year-round, but they are at their best from fall through winter and into spring. (It is no longer true that they may be eaten only in months with an "r" in them.) Purchase oysters at a market that has a heavy turnover of shellfish. If you gather them yourself, know the waters to be sure they are not polluted. Oysters should be bought live. You can tell they're alive if the shells are tightly closed. Select oysters that feel heavy, with shells intact and odor as fresh as a sea breeze. They may keep for a couple of days in the coldest part of the refrigerator but are best consumed on the day of purchase. If you must buy shucked oysters, be sure of your fishmonger and consume very promptly.

OYSTER PLANT
See SALSIFY.

P

PANCAKE SYRUP
See CORN SYRUP, MAPLE SYRUP.

PAPAYA

Available throughout the year, the papaya is at its peak in the spring. This fairly large, pear-shaped fruit grows on trees and tastes somewhat like a melon. Green when picked, papaya turns golden yellow in color at maturity, but the fruit is found at the market in varying degrees of ripeness. The length of time required to ripen at home varies according to the color of the skin. For example, fruit that is 25 to 35 percent yellow will take approximately two to four days to ripen at room temperature. When ready to eat, the papaya should be mostly to fully yellow and yield to gentle pressure. A ripe papaya has a fruity aroma. The skin should be smooth, unbruised, and unbroken. Avoid any shriveled or overly soft fruit. If desired, the home-ripening process may be speeded up by placing papayas in a paper bag and checking often until they reach their golden maturity. Once fully ripened, papayas will keep in the refrigerator for up to a week.

PAPRIKA

This colorful spice is derived from the red bell pepper. It should be kept with other dried herbs and spices in a cool, dark cupboard or pantry. Do not expose to light and especially not to sources of heat, such as a stove. Paprika is particularly prone to absorbing moisture from the air. Keep the container tightly closed at all times and refrigerate in the summer. Paprika should retain its potency for about six months. Fading color and aroma are sure signs that the spice is over the hill. A small, self-adhering label indicating date of purchase will help to keep track of shelf life.

PARSLEY

Fresh parsley is commonly sold in bunches throughout the year in both the familiar curly variety and the flat-leafed type called **Italian parsley**. Either way, it should have a fresh, green appearance. Avoid wilted or yellowing leaves. If the stems are immersed in water, be sure that the water is also fresh-looking and -smelling. Rinse thoroughly to rid the parsley of dirt, and pat dry with a paper towel. Place the parsley in a drinking glass with stems immersed in about two inches of water, then cover loosely with a plastic bag. Kept in the refrigerator in this manner, the parsley should stay fresh for up to a week or more. Check the water occasionally and replace if cloudy. Do not keep parsley in the coldest part of the refrigerator, where it may become frostbitten. For longest storage, chop parsley, dry thoroughly, place in a plastic bag, and freeze for up to six months or more.

Dried parsley flakes should be kept with other dried herbs and spices in a cool, dark cupboard or pantry. Do not expose to light and especially not to sources of heat, such as the stove. Keep the container tightly closed at all times. Dried parsley, under these conditions, should retain potency for up to a year. When the bright green color of the parsley becomes pale and dull, it is probably over the hill. A good sniff for the characteristic smell of the herb is also a useful check on its freshness. A small, self-adhering label indicating date of purchase will help to keep track of the shelf life of the dried parsley.

PARSNIP

Parsnips are available year-round, but the best (sweetest) are to be found in the winter and early spring. This pale, cream-colored cousin of the carrot should be firm and well shaped, free from straggly rootlets and fairly smooth. Smallish to medium-size parsnips are likely to be better than large ones, which may have a woody core. Avoid any that appear limp or shriveled. The green tops (if any) are not edible but should have a sprightly, fresh appearance. Discard the tops and refrigerate parsnips in a plastic bag in the crisper, where they will keep, depending on basic quality of the vegetable, for anywhere from one to four weeks.

PASSION FRUIT (GRANADILLA)

Named because its flower symbolized the Passion of Jesus Christ to early Spanish missionaries, passion fruit looks like a wrinkled, purple egg. This tropical fruit is a rarity in most markets but may be found in some areas during its July to November season. Look for large, firm fruit that feels heavy for its size. The more puckered the skin, the riper the fruit. Store ripe passion fruit in the refrigerator for up to a week.

PASTA

Spaghetti, linguine, fettucine, macaroni, egg noodles—the list of pasta varieties goes on and on. Whatever their shape or size, most pastas are simply flour and water, though egg noodles obviously include eggs in the formula as well. There is little one can do to detect freshness in a package of dried pasta other than to be sure the package has not been violated and that the place of purchase is one with high turnover of these products. Most dried pastas will keep on a kitchen shelf for several months without undue deterioration. For longer storage, transfer pasta to a tightly sealed glass or plastic container and keep in a dark, dry cabinet for up to a year. Egg noodles, under these conditions, will keep for up to six months. Fresh pasta is much more perishable; be sure that it was indeed made fresh very recently. Keep refrigerated and use within a day or two.

PEA

Fresh peas may be found throughout the year but are at their best when purchased locally during their peak season of late spring and early summer. The most common are called **English peas**, but flat **Chinese snow peas** and the newer, medium-size **sugar snap peas** are also popular. The pods of the larger English peas are discarded, while those of the other varieties are usually eaten with the peas themselves. In all cases, look for crisp, full pods of good green color and velvety texture. Avoid any that are limp or yellowing. Preshelled peas offer convenience but not the freshness or nutritive value of peas in the pod. Because their sugar quickly turns to starch, peas should be consumed promptly. If they must be stored, keep in a plastic bag in the refrigerator for a day or two and shell just before using.

PEA BEANS
See BEANS, DRIED.

PEACH
At their peak in the summer, peaches may be found year-round. The best indicator that a peach is ripe is that its ground (background) color is yellowish or creamy. Don't look at the blush or reddish color, which is present in varying degrees on every peach. This has to do with the variety of the peach, not its ripeness. A green ground color suggests that the peach was immature when picked and will not ripen after you bring it home. A ripe fruit will also have a distinctive "peachy" smell. The fresh, ripe peach is firm but not hard and should be free from blemishes and have an unwrinkled skin. Select peaches that are firm but give just a little when squeezed very gently. The softer ones may be eaten out of hand; otherwise refrigerate immediately. Store these fully ripe peaches in the refrigerator, spread out in one layer to minimize bruising, and use within a week. Allow the firmer ones to ripen at room temperature, spread evenly on a counter, away from sunlight, or in a loosely closed paper bag.

PEANUT
Peanuts in the shell should be clean and free from cracks and punctures. The peanuts themselves should not rattle around in their shells. To maintain the best eating quality, peanuts need protection from high temperatures. Because of their high fat content, peanuts are susceptible to rancidity in extreme heat. Store peanuts in a cool, dry place, preferably at 70°F or less, and they will keep for up to a month. It is recommended for prolonged freshness that peanuts be refrigerated or frozen. In the shell, peanuts keep approximately nine months in the refrigerator and keep indefinitely if frozen in a tightly closed container at 0°F or lower. Shelled peanuts in a tightly closed container keep approximately six

months in the refrigerator and up to five years if frozen at 0°F. Unopened, vacuum-packed peanuts will keep indefinitely on the kitchen shelf. *Moldy peanuts may be carcinogenic and should be discarded.*

PEANUT BUTTER

Like peanuts, peanut butter (both smooth and chunky) should be stored in a cool, dry place, ideally at 70°F or cooler. Under these conditions, an unopened jar should remain fresh for two to four years. After opening, the peanut butter may still be kept on a kitchen shelf for up to three months, but the flavor will begin to deteriorate after that period. If these conditions cannot be met, refrigeration is recommended for up to three or four months. The lid should be sealed tightly so there will be no chance of the peanut butter picking up moisture from the air. Refrigeration will also tend to make the peanut butter more difficult to spread. Freezing peanut butter is not advised, because of oil separation and other textural changes. If even a trace of mold appears, discard.

PEANUT OIL
See OIL, COOKING.

PEAR

Since pears do not ripen properly on the tree, they are harvested when they are quite hard. Commercial cold storage then keeps pears from ripening too quickly, making them available all year-round. The trick is to select firm, clear-skinned fruit that has not fully ripened and then complete the ripening process at home. Select pears that are free from bruises, cuts, or punctures and that do not give when pressed gently in the palm of the hand. Like many other fresh fruits, pears produce a natural gas called ethylene during the ripening process. To hasten this natural process, place several pears in a loosely closed paper bag or ripening bowl left at room temperature for several days. Check the pears daily. Since pears ripen from the inside out don't wait until they are very soft to the touch, because the inside may by then be too mushy. When they are fragrant and yield slightly to gentle palm pressure, they are ripe and ready to eat. Store ripe pears in a plastic bag in the refrigerator, where they will keep for up to five days. The most popular pear varieties are **Bartlett** (green when picked, yellow when ripe); **Anjou** (they remain green); **Bosc** (brown); and **Comice** (light green, mottled, sometimes with red blush). Handling and storage is essentially the same for all of them.

PEAR APPLE
See ASIAN PEAR.

PECANS
Pecans may be purchased year-round. To select nuts in the shell that are of the highest quality, choose those that are clean and free from cracks and other surface damage. There is no correlation between the quality of a nut and its size. When selecting shelled pecans, look for plump nutmeats that are fairly uniform in color. The best ones have a golden brown color. You can store unshelled pecans in a cool, dry place for about two months. Unshelled pecans resist insects and aging much longer than shelled nuts. Both shelled and unshelled pecans may be kept under refrigeration in airtight containers for about nine months or stored in the freezer for up to two years. See also NUTS.

PEPINO
A member of the melon family, the pepino is imported from New Zealand and is available on a limited basis in late winter and spring. Look for smooth, vividly colored yellow skin streaked with pinkish purple, free from cuts and bruises. The

ripe pepino will yield to gentle pressure and will keep for a
week or so in the refrigerator.

PEPPER (HOT)
Hot peppers, or **chili peppers**, come in a great variety of
shapes, sizes, and colors, and at least some of them are available year-round. Unlike the larger sweet peppers, they tend
to be small, tapered, and of various colors, including green,
red, and yellow or combinations thereof. They often have
exotic names like **jalapeño**, **serrano**, **cayenne**, and **tabasco**.
In general, the smaller the chili pepper, the hotter it will be.
*All of these hot peppers need to be handled with great caution
in preparation. Use of rubber gloves and avoidance of touch-
ing the face, especially the eyes, are highly recommended.*
The peppers, like their sweet cousins, should be well shaped
and firm, with good glossy color. Avoid those with pale, soft,
pliable flesh. Store in the crisper in a brown paper bag for
up to a week.

PEPPER (PEPPERCORN)
This most popular of all spices is most commonly black or
white and may come as whole peppercorns (the dried berry
of the pepper plant) or in crushed or powdered form. It should
be kept with other dried herbs and spices in a cool, dark
cupboard or pantry. Do not expose to light and especially
not to sources of heat, such as a stove. Keep the container
tightly closed at all times. Ground pepper loses its pungency
rather quickly; it may keep for no more than a month or two.
Fading color and aroma are sure signs that the ground version
is over the hill. Whole peppercorns are much to be preferred;
they can last for years. A small, self-adhering label indicating
date of purchase will help to keep track of shelf life.

PEPPER (SWEET)

The common sweet pepper is often referred to as a **bell pepper** because of its shape, and is usually green in color. An unripe green pepper, however, will turn bright red if left on the vine, and other colors ranging from vivid yellow to an almost black purple are also sold throughout the year. Still another type of sweet pepper is the more elongated **frying (or Italian) pepper**, which may be light green or yellow or even red in color. Whatever the variety, look for well-shaped, thick-walled, firm peppers with a uniform glossy color. Pale skin and soft, pliable flesh indicate immaturity. Avoid waxed peppers if possible, as the coating may be easily removed only through roasting. Store in the crisper in a brown paper bag for one to two weeks. Green peppers will tend to stay fresh longer than the more mature red ones.

PEPPER SAUCE

Unopened, hot pepper sauces, such as Tabasco, will keep almost indefinitely on a cool, dry, dark kitchen shelf. They do not require refrigeration after opening but should not be kept beyond a year or if they turn brown, whichever occurs first.

PEPPERMINT

See MINT.

PEPPERONI

See SAUSAGE.

PERSIMMON

This sweet and unusual fall fruit looks something like a tomato, though it grows on trees. Its peak season is from October to December. Look for firm, plump, smooth-skinned, and highly colored fruit with fresh, green cap intact. The color is a brilliant red orange. An unripe persimmon is extremely astringent, so be sure to let the fruit ripen fully (and then some) at room temperature until it yields to gentle pressure. Ripening will accelerate if the fruit is placed in a paper bag with an apple. Oddly enough, if a hard, unripe persimmon is frozen and thawed the next day, it will emerge fully ripe! If not consumed at once, room temperature–ripened persimmons may be refrigerated but for no more than a day or two.

PHEASANT

Farm-raised pheasant is available in some urban markets but is most likely to be found frozen. It requires the same care in selection and storage as any poultry (see CHICKEN and TURKEY). If fresh, the pheasant should be meaty and plump with clear, unbroken skin and no off odor. Smaller birds are likely to be young and therefore more tender than larger ones. Refrigerate promptly and use the same day or next. If frozen, be sure the bird is frozen solid with no accumulation of fluid in the package to indicate the pheasant was frozen and thawed. It will keep for several more months in the freezer. Always thaw a frozen pheasant completely in the refrigerator before cooking.

PICKLE

Pickles in jars from the supermarket shelf will store well for up to a year in your kitchen in a cool, dark, dry place. Once opened, they must be refrigerated and resealed tightly after each use. They will keep well for a month or more. Fresh dill pickles, which are refrigerated when you buy them, should be in clear water. They must also be refrigerated at home and consumed before the "use by" date on the label.

PIE

For maximum freshness, pies from a bakery should be purchased within a day or two at most from the time they were

baked. (Get to know your baker.) As for commercially packaged pies, check for and heed the "sell by" date, if any.
Unless the pie is still well sealed in its original container, in-
vert a paper plate or an aluminum pie plate over the pie, wrap
in plastic, and refrigerate. Most pies will keep reasonably
well for up to a week; those with whipped cream or custard
fillings or those made without preservatives, for no more than
two days.

PIGNOLIA
See PINE NUT.

PIMIENTO
On a cool, dry, dark kitchen shelf, canned or jarred pimientos will keep almost indefinitely. Once opened, transfer (if
canned) both pimientos and liquid to a tightly sealed glass
jar and refrigerate for up to ten days.

PINE NUT
Also popularly known as **pignolias**, these nuts are commonly used in Italian and other Mediterranean cuisines. They
are almost always sold commercially in jars or plastic bags
and should be refrigerated. Once opened, they will keep there
for about a month. Freezing will prolong their life up to six
months.

PINEAPPLE
Pineapples are in their peak season from March to June but
are rushed to market in refrigerated ships throughout the year.
The best are flown in from Hawaii. It's not always easy to
tell a fresh, ripe pineapple by its appearance. The outer shell
varies in color from gold to brown to green. Look for large
fruit with a heavy "feel" and a crown of fresh green leaves.
If leaves are wilted or browning, the pineapple may be over
the hill. Sniff the bottom of the pineapple; if ready to eat, it

will give off a sweet aroma characteristic of the fruit. If the bottom is soft or oozing liquid, eschew! Pineapples will soften at room temperature but not sweeten further once they have been picked, so use soon after purchase, preferably within one to two days. Refrigeration is not recommended, but if absolutely necessary, a pineapple may keep for several days there wrapped in plastic.

PINTO BEANS
See BEANS, DRIED.

PISTACHIO
Pistachio nuts may be purchased throughout the year. The inner seed is typically green, while the naturally dull gray shell is often dyed red. Pistachios are sold with the shell already split and partially open. Look for pistachios that are clean and free from cracks and other surface blemishes. Store in a tightly sealed container in the refrigerator for up to three months, in the freezer for up to a year. See also NUTS.

PLANTAIN
This large cousin of the banana is a staple in the tropics and can be found year-round, especially in markets catering to Hispanic communities. Unlike bananas, plantains are never eaten raw but are cooked like a vegetable. They have been called the potato of the tropics. A plantain looks like a large greenish banana with rough, blemished skin. They become more yellowish as they ripen and, like bananas, become black when overripe. Look for plantains that feel firm but not too hard and whose skins are not deeply bruised, gouged, or split. Again, like bananas, allow them to ripen at room temperature away from direct sunlight. Depending upon the stage of ripeness when purchased, they may keep for up to two weeks. Refrigeration as a last resort may preserve extremely ripe plantains for a day or two.

109

PLUM

Plums come in a bewildering variety of shapes, sizes, and colors, ranging from red to deep purple, from gold to bright green. Available from May into September, plums are at their peak from June through August. In selecting fresh plums, look for fruit that is richly colored for its variety, smooth of skin, and free from blemishes, breaks, and mold. Choose plums that are firm and plump. When ripe, plums give to gentle palm pressure and are slightly soft at the tip end. The light dusting on the skin called "bloom" occurs naturally and is nature's own protective coating. Like peaches, nectarines, and other fruits, plums give off ethylene gas which helps to complete the ripening process. If placed in a loosely closed paper bag or ripening bowl at room temperature, too firm plums will soften within a day or two. Plums should be refrigerated before washing. In a sealed plastic bag, they will keep for several days. Wash gently and serve at room temperature or slightly chilled.

So-called **fresh prunes** are distinguished from plums on rather technical grounds, but both are true plums. Dried prunes are the result of drying fresh prunes.

PLUM TOMATO
See TOMATO.

POI
See TARO.

POMEGRANATE

Pomegranates have a short fall season and are at their peak in October and November. Their juice is the source of the cocktail syrup called grenadine. Famed also for their multitude of seeds and the mess they tend to create when eaten, pomegranates are about the size of large apples and should have a tough, leathery rind that can vary in color from yellow to bright red (though more often of the latter hue). They are prized (and cursed!) for their seeds, which are enveloped in a brilliant red, juicy flesh. The fruit should be firm and feel heavy for its size; the rind should be relatively unblemished, free from cuts and gouges, and of good, bright color. Pomegranates can be kept for several days at room temperature or refrigerated for up to two weeks.

POPCORN
The freshest raw popcorn comes in a sealed jar with a tight-fitting screwtop lid. If it comes in a bag, be sure there are no tears or punctures and check to see if the product is sale-dated. Keep popcorn in an airtight container and store in a cool cupboard, where it should stay reasonably fresh for a year or more. Avoid refrigerating popcorn, because the air inside a refrigerator contains little moisture and can cause the popcorn to dry out. If you find you're getting too many "old maids" (kernels that don't pop), try adding a table-spoon of water to a one-quart jar three-quarters full of popcorn kernels. Close tightly and shake the jar off and on for several minutes until all the water has been absorbed, then store in a cool place. In a couple of days the kernels should again be quite poppable.

POPPY SEED
Available wherever dried herbs and spices are sold, poppy seeds should be kept in a cool, dark, dry place, away from light and heat. In a tightly sealed container, they will keep for several months. Because they contain oil, they are given to rancidity and will therefore keep even better, and considerably longer, in the refrigerator.

PORK
Universally available in various cuts, fresh pork should be light pink in color. Steak and roast cuts should have a firm

111

and lightly marbled texture. The fat should be white and firm. In appropriate cuts, the bones should be red on the ends. Avoid packages that are punctured or torn, or those with too much blood in them, which may indicate the meat has been frozen and thawed or has been on display too long. To store fresh pork, remove the original wrapping and wrap loosely in plastic or foil (tight wrapping tends to promote bacterial growth) and refrigerate for no more than three to four days. Store smoked pork in its original wrapper for up to two weeks in the refrigerator. See also BACON, HAM, SAUSAGE.

POTATO

Most readily available potatoes fall into four basic types: **russet**, **round red**, **long white**, and **round white**. The so-called new potato is actually nothing but an immature potato, usually on the small side, that has been shipped direct from field to market and not placed in prolonged storage. It may be either white or red. Regardless of shape, texture, or color, choose potatoes that are reasonably clean, very firm, and smooth. Try to select potatoes that are fairly regular in shape to avoid waste in peeling, and choose potatoes of uniform size for even cooking. Avoid potatoes with wilted, wrinkled skin, soft dark areas, or cut surfaces. A greenish cast to the skin does not indicate immaturity, but rather prolonged exposure to light, which gives potatoes a bitter taste. Ideally, potatoes should be stored in a cool, dark place that is well ventilated. At 45°–50°F, potatoes will keep well for several weeks, new potatoes for somewhat less time. At higher temperatures potatoes cannot be stored for much more than one week, new potatoes, again, for less time. Warm temperatures encourage sprouting and shriveling. (Sprouting potatoes needn't be discarded; if the potatoes are still firm, just cut out the sprouts.) Do not store potatoes near onions; something in the chemical interaction of the two vegetables can curtail the shelf life of both. Never refrigerate potatoes. At temperatures below 40°F, their natural starch begins to turn to sugar, lending them a sweet taste and causing them to darken when cooked. See also SWEET POTATO.

POTATO CHIPS
Since most potato chips are consumed in short order, the question of prolonged storage is rarely raised. If you must store chips after the bag is opened, however, they are best kept in an airtight, dry container, in which they will stay crisp and fresh for up to six weeks. If chips are exposed to moisture or high humidity, pop them briefly in a 350°F oven to restore their crispness.

PRAWN
See SHRIMP.

PRESERVES
Select a tightly sealed jar at the market and store for up to a year, unopened, on a cool, dry, dark kitchen shelf. Once opened, preserves and **conserves** (which are simply preserves made from more than one kind of fruit) will keep for about a month at room temperature, but refrigeration is recommended unless you expect to use up the preserves very quickly. If preserves are left on the shelf, always wipe clean around the lid so that no trace is left to attract insects. Refrigerated, preserves will keep for about six months. If mold forms on the surface, remove a thin layer that contains the mold and use the rest of the preserves fairly promptly.

PRICKLY PEAR
This pear-shaped berry, also called **cactus pear**, is about the size of a large egg. The fruit is the product of a number of cactus plants, with prickly spines removed before marketing. In flavor, it is often compared with watermelon. Prickly pears

113

are most available in the fall and early winter but are some-times to be found in the summer as well. Color ranges from green (unripe) through yellow to red (ripe). Look for colorful fruit with firm skin that yields slightly to pressure. Ripe prickly pears will keep for several days in the refrigerator.

PRUNE, DRIED
The dried prunes commonly sold in cardboard boxes or sealed plastic bags are dried fresh plums, which botanically are just another variety of plum. Not all varieties of plums become prunes, however. The ones that are used for prunes always have purple skin, are of the freestone type, and do not ferment as they dry. If you can't see what you're buying, shake the box to be sure that it doesn't rattle. Prunes should be relatively soft and moist. They will keep unopened on the kitchen shelf for up to six months. Once opened, prunes will keep in a tightly sealed container in the refrigerator for up to eight months. To plump up hardened prunes, cover with boiling water and refrigerate for twenty-four hours.

PRUNE, FRESH
See PLUM.

PUMPKIN
Pumpkins may be found throughout much of the year in some areas but are, of course, at their peak in the fall and early winter. Firm rind of clear color, free from blemishes, cracks, and gouges, is a must, as is a heavy feel in relationship to size. The pumpkin is a winter squash, all of which tend to be thicker-skinned than summer squash. A sharp rap on the rind of a pumpkin will provide a sense of how thick the skin is. If you can store a pumpkin at 50°F (perhaps in a garage or on a porch out of direct sunlight), it will last up to thirty days. At normal room temperature, it will keep for only about a week. Refrigeration is not recommended (let alone prac-

tical) unless temperature exceeds 70°F. See also SQUASH, WINTER.

PUMPKIN SEEDS
Heat, light, and dampness are the enemies of fresh pumpkin seeds. Store them in a cool, dark, dry place in an airtight container. They will keep there for several months, but because of the seeds' natural oil, refrigeration (especially in the summer) is preferred for longer storage of up to a year.

QUAIL
Farm-raised quail is now available in many urban markets, but in most places it is more likely to be found frozen. It requires the same care in selection and storage as any poultry (see CHICKEN and TURKEY). If fresh, the quail should be meaty and plump with clear, unbroken skin and no off odor. If the breastbone is soft and springy, the quail is probably a young and tender one. Smaller birds are also likely to be young and therefore more tender than larger ones. Refrigerate promptly and use the same day or next. If frozen, be sure the bird is frozen solid with no accumulation of fluid in the package to indicate the quail was frozen and thawed. Always thaw a frozen quail completely in the refrigerator before cooking.

QUINCE
The quince has been compared in appearance with a somewhat misshaped yellow apple. Quinces are available in the fall. Look for large, firm, golden fruit with smooth, unblemished skin. Too tart to be eaten raw, they are usually used in jams and jellies. Handle gently, because quinces bruise eas-

ily. They will keep well in a cool, dry place or refrigerator crisper for many weeks.

RABBIT
Rabbit may be available fresh in some butcher shops but is more likely to be found frozen. If fresh, select a plump, meaty animal with clear, unblemished, pinkish flesh and no off odor. Refrigerate promptly and use the same day or next. If frozen, be sure the rabbit is frozen solid with no accumulation of fluid in the package to indicate it was frozen and thawed. It will keep for at least six months in the freezer. Always thaw a frozen rabbit completely in the refrigerator before cooking.

RADICCHIO
Most radicchio is imported from Italy. It is similar in its bitterish flavor to Belgian endive but very different in shape and color. The small, round, compact heads are reddish purple in color, streaked with white. Popular as a trendy salad ''green,'' radicchio is available year-round in specialty food outlets. Select leaves that are colorful, crisp, light-textured, and free from wilting or discoloration. Store up to a week in a sealed plastic bag in the refrigerator and wash just before using.

RADISH
Radishes are available throughout the year, but the common red, globular radish is at its peak and at its best in late spring and early summer. In addition to the red, there are white and black radishes. Increasingly popular is the long, white Japanese **Daikon radish**. All of them should be firm, crisp, well

formed, and free from excessive black spots. Avoid radishes that feel spongy or those that are cracked and gouged. If greens are attached, they should have a sprightly, fresh appearance with no sign of yellowing and wilting. Remove the greens before storing and refrigerate in a plastic bag for up to two weeks. Like celery, limp radishes will perk up after a brief bath in ice water. See also HORSERADISH.

RAISIN
Because raisins are so sweet that microorganisms cannot survive in them, they need no preservatives. Controlled, cool storage is the best way to keep raisins. Heat and air can cause raisins to dry out, and humid conditions will cause the sugar in the fruit to crystallize. Therefore, after the package has been opened, raisins should be put in a sealed container or a plastic bag and refrigerated. Raisins will keep for up to two years if stored in the refrigerator. They can be kept even longer if frozen. Raisins will thaw quickly at room temperature. If raisins have formed sugar crystals or become dry due to improper storage, rinse them in hot tap water to dissolve the crystals and restore the moisture.

RASPBERRY
This most fragile and most costly of berries is at its peak of flavor and freshness in June, July, and August but is also available in some places through the fall. Raspberries should be purchased in half-pint containers; in larger quantities the berries press down upon each other and cause bruising. Examine raspberries carefully. They should have a bright, clear, even red color. Look for berries that are dry, plump, and well formed. Avoid those that still have green caps attached, as that indicates they were picked too early. There should be no sign of mold, rot, and bruising or of seeping juices on the container. If you can't eat them the same day, gently (very gently) pick over the berries, discarding any that are too soft

or moldy, and store the remainder, unwashed, for no more than another day or two in the refrigerator. Spread the berries in a single layer on a paper towel and cover lightly with plastic wrap. Wash, again gently, just before using.

RELISH
Relishes will keep unopened on a cool, dark, dry shelf for up to a year. Once opened, they must be tightly sealed and stored in the refrigerator, where they will keep for up to two months.

RHUBARB
Rhubarb can be found much of the year, from January through August. Outdoor-grown (as opposed to hothouse-grown) rhubarb comes into season in the spring and remains available through the summer. Look for firm, crisp, tender stalks of medium size; large stalks may be tough. They should be of good, bright color, ranging from cherry red to pink. *The leaves contain oxalic acid, a poison, and should never be eaten.* Use promptly, or store stalks, wrapped in plastic, in the refrigerator crisper for up to one week.

RICE
White rice, whether converted or instant, keeps almost in-definitely in its original sealed container without refrigeration. Once the box is opened, the rice should be stored in a tightly sealed container that keeps out moisture, dust, and other contaminants. Brown rice, on the other hand, because of the oil in the bran layers left on the grain, will keep un-opened no more than six months on the shelf and only about two months after that in a tightly sealed canister. Refrigeration of brown rice is recommended in warm, humid weather. When in doubt, refrigerate promptly after opening the original package. Wild rice, which isn't really a rice at all but rather the seed of a grass that grows underwater in some parts

of the United States, will also keep almost indefinitely on the shelf, but like true rice, it should be sealed tightly once the package is opened. If even a trace of mold appears on any rice, discard.

RICOTTA
See CHEESE.

ROCK CORNISH GAME HEN
See CHICKEN.

ROCKET
See ARUGULA.

ROLLS
See BREAD.

ROQUEFORT
See CHEESE.

ROSEMARY
Fresh rosemary is not commonly found in retail outlets but does show up in some supermarkets and gourmet stores. Look for fresh-appearing bunches of this dark, green-needled, highly aromatic herb, with no yellowing or wilting of the leaves. Rinse thoroughly and pat dry with a paper towel. Kept sealed in a plastic bag in the refrigerator, rosemary will stay fresh for up to a week. For longer storage, place rosemary leaves, chopped and thoroughly dried, in a small plastic bag and freeze up to six months or more. Dried rosemary leaves should be kept with other dried herbs and spices in a cool, dark cupboard or pantry. Do not expose to light and especially not to sources of heat, such as the stove. Keep the container tightly closed at all times. Dried rosemary leaves, under these conditions, should retain some po-

tency for up to a year, dried ground rosemary for up to six months. When the green color of the rosemary becomes pale and dull, the herb is probably over the hill. A good sniff for the characteristic smell of rosemary is also a useful check on its freshness. A small, self-adhering label indicating date of purchase will help to keep track of shelf life.

RUTABAGA
This large, yellow-fleshed cousin of the turnip is available throughout the year. It is often called a **yellow turnip**. The best are found from October through July. Rutabagas are usually coated with wax to preserve their moistness; this can simply be peeled off before using. The vegetable should be firm and smooth and feel heavy for its size. Smaller is usually better, as the largest rutabagas are apt to have woody, fibrous centers. Avoid rutabagas with cracks or gouges in the skin. Stored in a plastic bag in the refrigerator crisper, they will keep for up to two weeks.

SAFFLOWER OIL
See OIL, COOKING.

SAGE
Fresh sage is not commonly found in retail outlets but does show up in some supermarkets and gourmet stores. Select a fresh-appearing bunch with gray-green leaves intact. Avoid wilted or yellowing sage. Rinse thoroughly and pat dry with a paper towel. Kept sealed in a plastic bag in the refrigerator, sage will stay fresh for up to a week. For longest storage, place chopped and thoroughly dried sage leaves in small plastic bags and freeze for up to six months or more. Dried

sage leaves should be kept with other dried herbs and spices in a cool, dark cupboard or pantry. Do not expose to light and especially not to sources of heat, such as the stove. Keep the container tightly closed at all times. Dried sage leaves, under these conditions, should retain some potency for up to a year, dried ground sage for up to six months. When the typical gray-green color of the sage becomes pale and dull, the herb is probably over the hill. A good sniff for the characteristic smell of sage is also a useful check on its freshness. A small, self-adhering label indicating date of purchase will help to keep track of the shelf life of the dried sage.

SALAD DRESSING
Processed salad dressings will last for a year or more, unopened, on a kitchen shelf away from sources of light and heat. Once opened, they should be refrigerated and returned promptly to the refrigerator after each use. Tightly sealed, they will keep there for up to six months. If the dressing was refrigerated at point of purchase, it most likely does not contain preservatives and should therefore be refrigerated immediately at home. Leftover homemade salad dressings should be refrigerated and used within a few days.

SALAMI
See SAUSAGE.

SALSIFY
It is said that this root vegetable's flavor resembles that of oysters; hence its common name of **oyster plant**. It looks something like a parsnip. The root itself is slim and grayish white in color, with firm, juicy, white flesh. Because salsify discolors quickly when cut, rub cut surfaces immediately with lemon juice. Hardly a common item in food stores, salsify can more easily be found in fall and winter. The roots

should be firm and free from soft spots, cuts, or cracks. Store in the refrigerator in a plastic bag for up to two weeks.

SALT

Table salt is usually iodized and often has other additives. The coarser kosher salt is not so fine-grained but contains no additives. Either way, salt keeps indefinitely on a kitchen shelf. Seasoned salt is subject to deterioration, however; it may be kept in a cool, dark, dry place for up to one year.

SALT PORK
See BACON.

SAPOTE

Also called **Mexican custard apple**, this tropical fruit looks like a green apple with no indentation on the bottom. It may be found in some retail outlets, especially those catering to large Hispanic populations. Look for clear green or yellowish green color and firm flesh that is free from bruises and cuts. Let the sapote ripen at room temperature until it softens (which may take no more than a day) and yields to gentle pressure, then consume or refrigerate for several days.

SAUSAGE

Sausage may be purchased either precooked or uncooked; the latter is particularly perishable. Look for well-sealed packages with no tears or punctures and for sausage that appears firm, moist, and appealing to the eye. If you can smell it, the scent should appeal as well. Fresh, uncooked sausage such as common pork sausage and sweet or hot Italian sausage, well sealed, will keep for only a few days in the refrigerator; precooked sausages such as **hot dogs**, **bologna**, and **knockwurst** as well as brown-and-serve types will keep for up to a week beyond their "sell by" date. **Kielbasa** may be sold either fresh or precooked; it is most important to read the label or ask your grocer or butcher if there is any question about this or any other sausage. So-called dry sausages such as **salami** and **pepperoni** may be purchased whole in many groceries and delicatessens. They will keep up to a month or more in the refrigerator in whole form and for about two weeks once their casing has been cut.

SAVORY
A popular herb, savory may occasionally be found in fresh bunches in some retail outlets. Both **winter savory** and its close cousin, **summer savory** (which is considered the more delicate and desirable of the two), should have fresh-appearing dark green leaves and be free from yellowing or wilting. Rinse thoroughly and pat dry with a paper towel. Kept sealed in a plastic bag in the refrigerator, savory should stay fresh for about a week. For longer storage, up to six months or more, seal washed and thoroughly dried savory leaves in a small plastic bag and freeze. Dried savory, which comes in both crushed leaf and powdered form, should be kept with other dried herbs and spices in a cool, dark cupboard or pantry. Do not expose to light and especially not to sources of heat, such as a stove. Keep the container tightly closed at all times. Dried savory leaves, under these conditions, should retain some potency for up to a year, the powdered variety for up to six months. Fading color and aroma are sure signs that the herb is over the hill. A small, self-adhering label indicating date of purchase will help to keep track of shelf life.

SAVOY CABBAGE
See CABBAGE.

SCALLION
Commonly known as **green onions**, scallions are actually onions pulled from the soil before the full onion bulb has a

chance to develop. Scallions are available throughout the year but are at their freshest when locally grown and harvested in the spring and summer. Look for crisp bunches of scallions, with deep green, slightly bluish tops and clean white bulbs. Avoid any that are wilted, bruised, or yellowing. If the roots are not intact, the scallions will tend to dry out quickly. Wrap in plastic and keep in the vegetable crisper of the refrigerator. The greens may become slimy within a few days. If so, just cut them off; the bulbs should still be fresh and usable after a week or more.

SCALLOP
Like all shellfish, scallops are extremely perishable. Sea scallops, the larger variety, are at their best during the cooler months, and may be found fresh in areas where they are caught. In most markets, however, they have probably been frozen and thawed. The true bay scallop, the smaller variety, is available fresh only in the fall. You can usually tell that the scallops were frozen and thawed if the flesh has an opaque rather than translucent appearance. They should be firm, white (or pinkish in the case of bay scallops), dry (little or no liquid), and, most important, sweet-smelling. Avoid any with a strong ammoniated odor. Use promptly, storing no more than a day in the coldest part of the refrigerator.

SERRANO PEPPER
See PEPPER (HOT).

SESAME OIL
See OIL, COOKING.

SESAME SEED
Available wherever dried herbs and spices are sold, sesame seeds should be kept in a cool, dark, dry place, away from light and heat. In a tightly sealed container, they will keep

for several months. Because they contain oil, they are given to rancidity and will therefore keep even better, and considerably longer, in the refrigerator.

SHALLOT
This elegant and costly member of the onion family is available all year long but is likely to be of lesser quality during the hottest summer months. Its somewhat irregularly shaped bulbs grow in clusters and may be as small as a garlic clove or as large as a smallish onion. Shallots have a slightly reddish, tan-colored, papery skin, which should feel dry to the touch. Shallots should be firm and plump. Avoid any that are withered, shrunken, bruised, soft, or sprouting. Store them, like onions, in a dark cool, dry, well-ventilated place. If you use a kitchen cabinet, select one that is not adjacent to a stove, steam pipe, dishwasher, or other heat-producing instrument. They may keep for up to two months under ideal conditions, but shallots are likely to go soft or sprout much earlier than that if the air is warm and humid.

SHERBET
See ICE CREAM.

SHORTENING
Like lard, vegetable shortenings such as Crisco may be kept tightly sealed at room temperature on a cool, dry shelf for up to a year.

SHRIMP
Like all shellfish, shrimp are extremely perishable. Shrimp are available fresh year-round in areas where they are caught but will have been frozen and thawed in most markets. For freshest shrimp, buy at a fishmonger's that has a heavy turnover of shellfish. You can usually tell that the shrimp were frozen and thawed if the flesh has an opaque rather than a

125

translucent appearance. They should be firm, springy to the touch, well filled out within their shells, and, always, fresh-smelling. Color and size have little to do with quality. Avoid any with a strong ammoniated odor. Store in the coldest part of the refrigerator and consume on day of purchase. If you must keep longer, cook the shrimp immediately and store, again in the coldest part of the refrigerator, for two or three days at most. The closely related and very similar **prawn** (which may sometimes be sold as shrimp) requires the same handling and storage.

SNAP BEAN
See GREEN or WAX BEAN.

SNOW PEA
Snow peas are available year-round. Also known as **Chinese pea pods**, these are the popular flat pods that are eaten whole and often used in Chinese cuisine. They do have tiny peas inside, but the important thing to look for, as with all peas, is crispness, good green color, and velvety texture. Avoid any that are limp or yellowing. Use promptly or, if neces-sary, refrigerate in a plastic bag for no more than a day or two. Wash just before using. See also PEA.

SORREL
This sourish-tasting herb is also known as **dock**. It may be found in some specialty outlets throughout the year but is more common from February through November. It is used in salads and soups. The long, arrow-shaped leaves should have a fresh, light green appearance and be free from yel-lowing, limpness, and excessive dirt. Use promptly or store unwashed in a plastic bag in the refrigerator for no more than a day or two.

SOUR CREAM

Always heed the "sell by" date on the carton and select one that is tightly sealed and well chilled. Refrigerate promptly. Sour cream will keep in the refrigerator for about ten days. If liquid separates from the cream, simply pour it off; the sour cream itself will be fine. When serving sour cream at table, transfer what you need to a serving dish and promptly reseal and refrigerate the original carton.

SOY BEANS

See BEANS, DRIED.

SOY SAUCE

Unopened, this common Oriental condiment keeps for up to a year on a cool, dark, dry kitchen shelf. Some authorities say that it does not require refrigeration after opening, but the label of the popular Kikkoman brand does stipulate refrigeration. It certainly can't hurt. Soy sauce will keep well in the refrigerator for several months.

SPAGHETTI

Spaghetti, like most pastas, is nothing more than flour and water. There is little one can do to detect freshness in a package of dried spaghetti other than to be sure that the package has not been violated and that the place of purchase is one with high turnover of this product. Unopened, dried spaghetti will keep on a kitchen shelf for several months without undue deterioration. For longer storage, transfer spaghetti to a tightly sealed glass or plastic container and keep in a dark, dry cabinet for up to a year. Fresh spaghetti is much more perishable. Be sure that it was indeed made fresh very recently. Keep refrigerated and use within a day or two.

SPAGHETTI SQUASH

Named for its flesh, which, when cooked, separates into long, spaghettilike strands, this popular squash is available all year. It is bright yellow in color and elongated in shape. Its skin is not as hard as that of other winter squashes, but not as soft as that of summer squashes. The rind should still be fairly firm, and the squash should have a heavy feel for its size, indicating that it is moist inside. Look for a dull rather than shiny surface and a rind free from bruises, gouges, and soft or sunken spots. Spaghetti squash will keep for a week or so at normal room temperatures. In hot weather it may be refrigerated for up to two weeks.

SPEARMINT
See MINT.

SPICES AND HERBS

The distinction between a spice and an herb is somewhat technical, and opinions vary on just what it is. One authority states that herbs grow in temperate climates, spices in tropical, with the exception of bay, which grows in either. In terms of selecting and storing them, however, it makes little difference. One knows almost instinctively, for example, that parsley and tarragon are herbs and pepper and nutmeg are spices.

Fresh herbs, in general, should look fresh: have sprightly green leaves, be free from yellowing, wilting, and insect damage, and have an appealing aroma. They should be rinsed thoroughly and patted dry with a paper towel. Sealed in a plastic bag, they will keep for about a week in the refrigerator. Basil is an exception: it abhors cold and should be kept in a glass of water like flowers in a vase. Most fresh herbs may also be chopped, dried thoroughly, and kept in small plastic bags in the freezer for six months or more.

Many dried herbs and spices come in both whole and

ground form. The whole will last considerably longer than the ground, for up to a year as opposed to six months. Glass and tin containers are preferred over cellophane and plastic, which can let in air and hasten deterioration of the product. Purchase dried herbs and spices in the smallest available quantities, and keep tightly sealed in a cool, dark cabinet or pantry. Do not expose to light and especially not to sources of heat, such as a stove. Fading color and/or aroma are sure signs that the spice or herb is over the hill. A small, self-adhering label indicating date of purchase will help to keep track of shelf life.

See also specific spices and herbs.

SPINACH
Spinach is available year-round but is at its best in the cooler months. It may have either flat or the more familiar crinkly leaves. In either case, choose fresh, young, and well-colored spinach. Look for a dark green color, and avoid any spinach with large yellow leaves or those that are wilted, discolored, or slimy. Some dirt is to be expected, but avoid spinach that feels or appears excessively gritty. Spinach in cellophane bags may be fine, but loose spinach, because it can be examined carefully, is always to be preferred. Store unwashed in the refrigerator in a sealed plastic bag for no more than two or three days. Wash *very* thoroughly just before using.

SPROUTS
Sprouts may be found almost everywhere throughout the year. Most common are **mung bean** and **alfalfa sprouts**, but sometimes those from soy beans are available. The shorter the sprout, the more tender. Be sure they are moist and crisp, avoiding those that are limp, soggy, or browning. They should also have a fresh, nutty aroma. Store damp, but not waterlogged, sprouts in a plastic bag in the refrigerator, where they will keep for a week or more.

SQUASH, SUMMER

This category of thin-skinned squashes includes the most popular **zucchini**, or green squash; **yellow squash** (which comes in both straight and crookneck varieties); and the much rarer discus-shaped, scallop-edged **white squash**, which is also known as **patty-pan squash**. Yellow and green squash are available year-round but are at their peak of freshness in the summer. Look for firm vegetables. If squash is soft or pliable or squishy, it is not fresh. The skin should be of good color, free from gouges and soft spots, and shiny rather than dull. In general, small- to medium-size squash will be the tenderest. The larger the squash, the larger and tougher its seeds. Handle gently, because thin-skinned summer squash is easily bruised, and store in the refrigerator in a plastic bag for four to six days. See also CHAYOTE.

SQUASH, WINTER

Different varieties of winter squash are increasingly appearing on the market. The more common ones include **buttercup**, **butternut**, **acorn**, **Hubbard**, and **spaghetti squash**. The **pumpkin** is also included in the winter squash category. All may be found in the fall and winter. The most popular butternut and acorn squashes are available year-round in many areas but are at their peak in the fall. All of these squashes are characterized by firm, hard rinds. If the rind feels thin or soft, the squash was probably picked prematurely. The squash should also have a heavy feel for its size, indicating that it is not dried out and stringy inside. Also look for a dull rather than a shiny surface (just the opposite from summer squash), indicating that the squash was allowed to mature fully on the vine. Squash should be free from bruises, gouges, and soft or sunken spots. Winter squash will keep for a week or so at normal room temperature. In a cool, airy place, away from direct sunlight, with temperatures around 50°F, it will keep for one or more months. In hot weather, winter squash should be refrigerated and will keep for up to two weeks.

SQUID

Like its cousin the **octopus**, the squid is a many-tentacled saltwater creature that is highly prized in some cuisines. It may be found fresh in some fish markets, particularly in large coastal cities. As with fish, the eyes should be clear, the scent sweet and fresh. Refrigerate promptly and use on day of purchase or the next at the latest.

STAR FRUIT (CARAMBOLA)

This ridged tropical fruit is often sliced into five-pointed sections that resemble a starfish: hence its popular name. It is available year-round in limited supply but is at its peak in the fall and winter. The waxy outer skin deepens in color as it ripens. When star fruit is golden yellow and gives forth a flowery aroma, it is ready to eat. It may be ripened at room temperature, away from direct sunlight, and then refrigerated for up to a week.

STEAK SAUCE

Unopened steak sauces, such as Worcestershire, will keep almost indefinitely on a cool, dry, dark kitchen shelf. They do not require refrigeration after opening but should not be kept beyond a year.

STRAWBERRY

Strawberries are available year-round but are at their peak of flavor from April through June. They are highly perishable and should be consumed as soon after purchase as possible. They do not ripen further once they have been picked. Select berries with uniform, bright red color. Size of berry has little bearing on flavor, but do choose well-shaped, firm berries with their green caps intact. Avoid berries that seem dry or those with brownish caps. Avoid, too, a basket that is badly stained—berries may well be bruised and dripping. Also look for extensive signs of mildew, which is more often found at the bottom of the basket. Pick over the berries and discard any that are softened or bruised before refrigerating. If possible, store berries in a single layer for best preservation. They will keep for several days. Wash gently just before using; moisture hastens mold, so it is best not to wash before storing. Remove stems only after washing.

STRING BEAN
See GREEN or WAX BEAN.

SUGAR
Granulated sugar in a tightly sealed canister or other container will keep virtually forever. So will powdered or confectioners' sugar. If sugar gets damp, it may harden but can be returned to its original state by pounding with a hammer or breaking up in a blender or food processor. If you prefer to keep sugar in its original container, place the whole package inside a tightly sealed plastic bag, which will help to keep out not only moisture but insects as well. Sugar substitutes and **sweeteners** also keep indefinitely whether in solid or liquid form.

SUMMER SAVORY
See SAVORY.

SUMMER SQUASH
See SQUASH, SUMMER.

SUNCHOKE
See JERUSALEM ARTICHOKE.

SUNFLOWER OIL
See OIL, COOKING.

SUNFLOWER SEEDS
Heat, light, and dampness are the enemies of fresh sunflower seeds. Store them in a cool, dark place in an airtight container. They will keep there for several months, but because of the seeds' natural oil, refrigeration (especially in the summer) is preferred for longer storage of up to a year.

SWEET POTATO
There are two basic varieties of sweet potato available in the United States, the dry-meated and the moist-meated. The moist type is often referred to as a **yam**, but in fact this is a misnomer. The true yam belongs to an entirely different genus of plants and is rarely cultivated in the United States. The skin of the dry type is usually light yellowish tan, while the skin of the moist-fleshed varieties varies in color from whitish tan to brownish red. Whatever the variety, sweet potatoes are available year-round but are at their best in August, September, and October. Choose sweet potatoes that are thick, chunky, of medium size, and taper toward the ends. Avoid those with any sign of decay, as deterioration spreads rapidly. Even a small bruise may affect the flavor of the entire potato. Sweet potatoes should not be refrigerated. If you have a cool (55°–60°F), dry place to hold them, they will keep for several months, but if they must be kept at room temperature, use them within a week.

SWEETBREADS
See VARIETY MEATS.

SWEETENERS
See SUGAR.

SWISS CHARD
Available year-round, though somewhat less so during the summer, this leafy green is used as a cooked vegetable. Choose fresh, young, and crisp bunches of green leaves. Avoid any with coarse stems or wilted, yellowing leaves. There is also a red-leafed Swiss chard that may occasionally turn up in markets. Store in the refrigerator in a sealed plastic bag for no more than a couple of days. Wash just before using.

SYRUP
See CORN SYRUP, MAPLE SYRUP.

TABASCO PEPPER (FRESH)
See PEPPER (HOT).

TABASCO SAUCE
Unopened Tabasco and other hot pepper sauces will keep almost indefinitely on a cool, dry, dark kitchen shelf. They do not require refrigeration after opening but should not be kept beyond a year or if they turn brown, whichever occurs first.

TANGELO
The tangelo is a cross between a tangerine and a grapefruit and has a special sweet/tart flavor. There are several varieties of tangelo, including the **Orlando** and the **Mineola**. The Mineola (in season from January to April) is the smaller of the two, slightly flattened in shape, lighter in color, and with more seeds. The larger Orlando (in season from December to March) looks more like an orange than a tangerine, has

deep orange color and a distinctive knoblike formation at the stem end, and is reputed to be the most flavorful of the tangelos. Tangelos have tighter skins than tangerines and are not so easily broken into segments. Look for bright, glossy skin, free from blemishes, soft spots, and mold. A heavy "feel" in relationship to size indicates juiciness. Tangelos may be kept at room temperature, away from heat and direct sunlight, for up to a week and in the refrigerator vegetable crisper for two to three weeks.

TANGERINE

The true tangerine is a member of the mandarin orange family and is at its peak in the months of November, December, and January. Fresh tangerines should have a brilliant orange color. The pebbly-textured skin should be glossy and free from blemishes, soft spots, and mold. As with all citrus fruit, look for tangerines that feel heavy for their size, which indicates juiciness. A thin, loose-fitting skin and a puffy appearance are desirable. Tangerines can be easily peeled and segmented. The **murcott**, or honey tangerine, is a recent variety with deep orange color and sweet flesh, though it does not peel as easily as regular tangerines. All tangerines will keep well for a week or so at room temperature, away from heat and direct sunlight, and for several weeks in a sealed plastic bag in the refrigerator crisper.

TANGOR
See TEMPLE ORANGE.

TARO

Also known as **dasheen**, taro is a potatolike fibrous tuber that is grown in tropical regions. It is particularly associated with Hawaii, where it is made into the staple called **poi**, and may usually be found in areas with large Asian and Hispanic populations. Noted for its digestibility when cooked, *taro is* *also potentially poisonous and should never be eaten raw.* Large, firm tubers, free from gouges and bruises, will keep for several days in a cool, dry, dark place or wrapped in plastic in the refrigerator.

TARRAGON

Bunches of fresh tarragon may occasionally be found in some retail outlets throughout the year. Look for fresh-appearing green leaves that are free from yellowing and wilting. Rinse thoroughly and pat dry with a paper towel. Kept sealed in a plastic bag in the refrigerator, tarragon should stay fresh for about a week. For longer storage, up to six months or more, seal chopped and thoroughly dried tarragon leaves in a small plastic bag and freeze. Dried tarragon leaves should be kept with other dried herbs and spices in a cool, dark cupboard or pantry. Do not expose to light and especially not to sources of heat, such as a stove. Keep the container tightly closed at all times. Dried tarragon, under these conditions, should retain some potency for up to a year. When its color becomes pale and dull, the herb is probably over the hill. A good sniff for the characteristic smell of tarragon is also a useful check on its freshness. A small, self-adhering label indicating date of purchase will help to keep track of shelf life.

TEA

Regardless of the kind of tea, it is important to keep it from exposure to air, moisture, and food odors. Store all teas in tightly sealed containers on a cool, dark, dry shelf, away from herbs and spices. Tea bags are the most perishable (the first to lose their fresh flavor) and will keep well for only a few months. If possible, buy tea in tins or bulk from reliable retailers with heavy turnover of this product. If fresh when purchased, black teas will store well for as long as two years, green and oolong for one year, herbal teas for about six months. A thin, papery taste will signal when a tea is over the hill.

TEMPLE ORANGE

Also known as royal mandarins or **tangors**, temple oranges are a cross between a tangerine and an orange. They taste like a sweet orange but, like a tangerine, have loose-fitting skin and are easily segmented. They are rather large, red orange in color, and at their peak from December until April. Like oranges and tangerines, temples are best if their skin has a bright, glossy color and is free from blemishes, soft spots, and mold. Look for fruit that feels heavy in relationship to its size, for these will be the juiciest temples. Temples will keep for a week or so at room temperature in a well-ventilated space, away from heat and direct sunlight, and for several weeks in the crisper of the refrigerator.

THYME

Bunches of fresh thyme may be found occasionally throughout the year in supermarkets and gourmet retail stores. The small, bright green leaves should have a fresh appearance and be free from yellowing and wilting. Rinse thoroughly and pat dry with a paper towel. Kept sealed in a plastic bag in the refrigerator, thyme should stay fresh for about a week. For longer storage, up to six months or more, place washed and thoroughly dried thyme sprigs, stems and all, in a small plastic bag and freeze. Dried thyme leaves should be kept with other dried herbs and spices in a cool, dark cupboard or pantry. Do not expose to light and especially not to sources of heat, such as a stove. Keep the container tightly closed at all times. Dried thyme leaves, under these conditions, should retain some potency for up to a year, dried ground thyme for up to six months. When the green color of thyme becomes pale and dull, the herb is probably over the hill. A good sniff for the characteristic smell of thyme is also a useful check on its freshness. A small, self-adhering label indicating date of purchase will help to keep track of shelf life.

TOFU

This widely available, white custardy substance is the curd produced from soy bean milk, which is then pressed into large "cakes" and cut into smaller squares for marketing. Produce departments should keep it at least partially refrigerated. Look for firm, white tofu in water, and heed the "sell by" date, if any. Keep tofu in a covered container in the refrigerator and change water daily. It is quite perishable, so use within five days at the most. If a slimy film appears on tofu, discard.

TOMATILLO

Called **husk** or **ground tomato**, this small vegetable may be yellow green, bright green, or purplish green in color and is covered with a papery husk. The flavor is tart and similar to that of a green apple or plum. Tomatillos may be found in markets catering to large Mexican and Hispanic populations. Avoid overly soft or withered vegetables, and keep in a cool, dry, well-ventilated place for up to two weeks.

TOMATO

Tomatoes may be purchased year-round, but the freshest and best-tasting are those that are grown locally and sold at or very near their peak of ripeness. These have developed full flavor, texture, and color, either a bright red or red-orange depending upon the variety. Local field-grown tomatoes are very tender and must be handled gently. They are at their best during the late summer. Because fully or nearly ripe fruit (yes, the tomato is a fruit, not a vegetable) is so easily damaged, most tomatoes are picked at an earlier (yet mature) stage of development and shipped to market before they ripen fully. These so-called vine-ripened tomatoes should be firm,

138

free from cracks and blemishes, and fairly well formed with smooth skins. Sort tomatoes according to their degree of ripeness and use fully ripe fruit first. Partially green or pinkish vine-ripened tomatoes will continue to ripen on the countertop at temperatures of 55°–70°F, but keep them from direct sunlight. They will ripen more quickly in a brown paper bag with an apple in it. (Ripening is enhanced by ethylene gas released by the apple.) If tomatoes do not ripen at all under these conditions, chances are they were picked too soon and forced into an appearance of ripeness by means of temperature and ethylene gas. Unfortunately, it is hard to tell the difference between these forced tomatoes and true vine-ripened fruit without tasting them. If possible, do not refrigerate tomatoes. They quickly lose flavor at cold temperatures but may keep well enough for a day or two in the refrigerator if need be. Any tomato, however, will taste better at room temperature. Pale, pinkish tomatoes shipped in cellophane-wrapped packages are not likely to ripen any further at home.

Plum or **pear tomatoes** are generally used for cooking and are at their best when almost overripe. Tiny **cherry tomatoes** may be bright red or yellow and are usually ripe and ready to use when purchased.

TOMATO PASTE
See TOMATO SAUCE.

TOMATO PUREE
See TOMATO SAUCE.

TOMATO SAUCE
Unopened, a can of tomato sauce will keep on a cool, dry, dark kitchen shelf for a year or more. Once opened, refrigerate leftover sauce in a tightly sealed glass or plastic container for up to ten days. Sauce may pick up an unpleasant

metallic taste if left in the original can. **Tomato puree** and **tomato paste** require the same handling and storage.

TRIPE
Tripe is the inner lining of the stomach of a cow or other beef animal, and like all organ meats, it is highly perishable. Look for firm, white, moist, honey-combed, odorless tripe. Refrigerate as soon as possible and use within a day or two at most.

TRUFFLE
Unlike their mushroom cousins, these fungi grow under the ground and are difficult to find. They are also very expensive. Most common are black truffles from France and white truffles from Italy, both highly prized. Small, roughly round in shape, and undistinguished in appearance, truffles are available in specialty markets in the fall and winter. They should be firm, plump, and fragrant, free from mold and slime. Store fresh truffles buried in uncooked rice (to absorb moisture) in a covered jar in the refrigerator, where they will keep, depending on their freshness at purchase, for up to two weeks.

TURKEY
Highly perishable, poultry is among the most common sources of food poisoning. Be sure to buy your turkey from a market or butcher with heavy turnover of this product. Any bird with a hint of an off odor should be avoided. Look for a plump, fresh turkey with moist, pearly white skin; bluish or purple tones indicate that the turkey may have been deep-chilled (just short of freezing) for shipping and is therefore not 100 percent fresh. An accumulation of liquid in the wrapping is also a sign of overage. Store a fresh turkey or fresh turkey parts in the coldest area of the refrigerator for no more than a day or two before cooking. Giblets should always be

promptly removed from the bird and cooked the day of purchase. A frozen turkey should be thawed only in the refrigerator and cooked promptly thereafter. Always remove the stuffing from the cavity after cooking and store separately in a covered bowl.

TURMERIC

Virtually always sold in ground form, turmeric is the bright yellow ingredient in curries and other Eastern dishes. Store with other dried herbs and spices in a cool, dark cupboard or pantry. Do not expose to light and especially not to sources of heat, such as a stove. Keep the container tightly closed at all times. Ground turmeric may retain some potency for up to six months. Fading color and aroma are sure signs that the spice is over the hill. A small, self-adhering label indicating date of purchase will help to keep track of shelf life.

TURNIP

This common root vegetable is available year-round. The white turnip (as opposed to its yellow cousin, the **rutabaga**) does have pure white flesh with a purple crown. A turnip should be firm and smooth and free from cracks. If the greens are attached, they should have a fresh, sprightly appearance. Smaller is usually better, as large turnips may have woody, fibrous centers. The turnip should have a heavy feel for its size. For storage, remove the greens and place turnips in a plastic bag in the refrigerator crisper, where they will keep for about a week.

TURNIP GREENS

Available throughout the year, but primarily in the South, these leafy greens are actually the tops of the white turnip. Choose fresh, young, and crisp green leaves. Avoid any with coarse stems, wilted, yellowing leaves, or signs of insect damage. Keep in the refrigerator in a sealed plastic bag and use promptly, within a day or two. Wash just before using.

U

UGLI FRUIT
About the size of a grapefruit, the ugli fruit really lives up to its name. The peel is extremely rough and looks disfigured, with light green blemishes that turn orange as the fruit ripens. Ugli fruit will feel heavy for its size because of its high juice content. It is very juicy and has a sweet flavor somewhat like a combination of grapefruit and orange. Like other citrus fruit, ugli fruit will keep at room temperature for several days in a well-ventilated place, out of direct sunlight, and in the refrigerator crisper for up to two weeks. Look for ugli fruit in the winter at specialty markets.

V

VANILLA EXTRACT
Store vanilla extract along with dried herbs and spices on a cool, dark, dry shelf. The high alcohol content (up to 35 percent) acts as a preservative, keeping vanilla fresh literally for years. If sediment appears at the bottom of the bottle, simply shake to blend back into the liquid.

VARIETY MEATS
All variety or **organ meats** are extremely perishable and must be refrigerated at all times. If possible, purchase **liver**, **sweetbreads**, **brains**, **kidneys**, and **hearts** from a reliable and trusted butcher shop or get to know the butcher at your

142

supermarket to be sure you are obtaining the freshest-possible product. Variety meats should have a fresh, moist appearance with no drying about the edges, a glossy shine to the color, and no odor. Refrigerate promptly and use the day of purchase or next at the latest.

VEAL
The meat of a young calf, true veal should be no more than three months old at time of slaughter. It is found all year but more abundantly in late winter and spring. Older calf meat is sometimes sold as veal but is more properly called young beef. You can usually tell real veal by its pale, pinkish white color. Older "veal" will have a darker red color. Veal should appear moist, glossy, firm, fine-textured. Avoid any veal in a torn package or one with an accumulation of blood in it; meat in the latter may have been frozen and thawed or may simply have been sitting too long in its tray. There should be little if any marbling in the meat, and the bones, if visible, should appear porous and reddish. Rewrap veal at home if you are not planning to use it that day, and wrap loosely so that air may circulate around the meat. Be careful lest drippings that might contain harmful bacteria fall on other foods or refrigerator shelves. Larger roast cuts and thick chops will keep for about three days in the refrigerator, thin scaloppine or cutlets and ground veal for no more than a day or two at most.

VEGETABLE OIL
See OIL, COOKING.

VEGETABLE PEAR
See CHAYOTE.

VINEGAR

Unopened, vinegar will keep almost indefinitely on a cool, dry, dark kitchen shelf. Once opened, most vinegars, if re-sealed tightly after using, will keep on that same shelf for about six months. Special vinegars, like wine and herb, are more perishable and should be used within about three months. Sediment at the bottom of the bottle does not indicate spoilage, but mold on the surface does. In the latter case, discard.

WALNUT

The usual variety of walnut found in markets is the **English walnut**, and it is available both in the shell and shelled year-round. The **black walnut**, a native American species, is noted for its extremely hard shell and is rarely sold commercially. Unshelled walnuts should be clean and free from cracks and other surface blemishes. If the shell rattles when shaken, the kernel is likely to be dried out. Stored in a cool, dry, dark place, unshelled walnuts will stay fresh for several months. Shelled walnuts should be refrigerated in a tightly sealed container and will keep for six months or more or for up to a year in the freezer. See also NUTS.

WALNUT OIL
See OIL, COOKING.

WATER CHESTNUT

Fresh water chestnuts may be found in some retail outlets, especially in the spring, in areas with large Asian populations. These blackish or brown-skinned, chestnut-shaped bulbs should be firm and plump, with no sign of mold. They will keep, unpeeled, in the refrigerator for about a week. Once canned water chestnuts are opened, they should be transferred to a covered glass or plastic container and kept in water, which should be changed daily. They will also keep in this way for about a week.

WATERCRESS
This plant grows in the wild along stream banks, but because it is also grown commercially, it is widely available throughout the year. Its flavor is most often described as "peppery." It is commonly used as a salad accent or a garnish. Look for bunches of dark green, crisp leaves with no trace of yellowing. Watercress is quite perishable, so store immediately in the refrigerator in a plastic bag and use within a day or two of purchase. Wash just before using.

WATERMELON
The aptly named watermelon (92 percent on average) may be found during most months of the year but is at its peak, and its best, in June, July, and August. It is hard to judge this book by its cover. The rind may vary in color and may or may not be striped, but the lower half of the watermelon, the part that rested on the ground as the melon developed, should be yellowish or creamy as opposed to green or white. A mature melon will also have a dull rather than a shiny surface. Cut watermelon should display a deep red color and firm, juicy flesh with no white streaks. Seeds vary in color but should be fully mature and hard. Uncut melons will keep at room temperature for several days; cut melon, tightly wrapped in plastic, will keep in the refrigerator for several days as well.

WAX BEAN
The **green bean** and its yellow cousin, the wax bean, are, except for color, interchangeable, and both are available

throughout the year. They are also known as **snap beans** or **string beans** (though the inedible "string" has long since been bred out of them). Whether yellow or green, look for bright, clear color, a velvety texture, and especially for a bean that really snaps when bent. A limp or wilting (overage) bean won't snap. Select long, straight, slender pods with small seeds. Beans that have begun to ridge and bulge will be tough. Use promptly or refrigerate for no more than two or three days in a plastic bag. Wash just before using.

WHEAT GERM
This is the heart of the wheat kernel, rich in nutrients. It is also rich in fat and thus prone to rancidity. Buy wheat germ in vacuum-packed jars and keep on a cool, dry, dark shelf for eight to twelve months. Once opened, always reseal tightly and store wheat germ in the refrigerator, where it will keep for up to six months.

WHITE SQUASH
See SQUASH, SUMMER.

WILD RICE
Wild rice isn't really a rice at all but the seed of a grass that grows underwater in some parts of the United States. Like true rice, it will keep almost indefinitely on the shelf in its original package but should be tightly sealed in a canister or other container once the package is opened and will keep there for about a year. See also RICE.

WINTER SAVORY
See SAVORY.

WINTER SQUASH
See SQUASH, WINTER.

WITLOOF
See BELGIAN ENDIVE.

WORCESTERSHIRE SAUCE
Unopened, Worcestershire and other steak sauces will keep almost indefinitely on a cool, dry, dark kitchen shelf. They do not require refrigeration after opening but should not be kept beyond a year.

YAM
See SWEET POTATO.

YEAST
Dry yeast is usually sold in small packets with "use by" dates on them. Store them in a cool, dry place and do not keep beyond the recommended date. So-called fresh or compressed yeast comes in small cake form; it should be refrigerated and used promptly.

YELLOW SQUASH
Yellow squash comes in both straight and crookneck varieties. It is available year-round but at its peak of freshness in the summer. Look for firm vegetables. If squash is soft or pliable or squishy, it is not fresh. The skin may be smooth or pebbly but should be of good color, free from gouges and soft spots, and shiny rather than dull. In general, small to medium-size squash will be the tenderest. The larger the squash, the larger and tougher its seeds. Handle gently, because thin-skinned summer squash is easily bruised, and store in the refrigerator in a plastic bag for four to six days.

EAT WELL...
LIVE WELL